ISBN: 9781314391510

Published by:
HardPress Publishing
8345 NW 66TH ST #2561
MIAMI FL 33166-2626

Email: info@hardpress.net
Web: http://www.hardpress.net

THE REAL CHARLOTTE

Rose Helps
From V. M.

June. 1894.

THE
REAL CHARLOTTE

BY

E. Œ. SOMERVILLE & MARTIN ROSS

AUTHORS OF

" AN IRISH COUSIN," "NABOTH'S VINEYARD," ETC.

IN THREE VOLUMES

VOL. I.

LONDON

WARD AND DOWNEY LTD.

12 YORK STREET COVENT GARDEN W.C.

1894

THE REAL CHARLOTTE.

VOLUME I.

CHAPTER I.

AN August Sunday afternoon in the north side of Dublin. Epitome of all that is hot, arid, and empty. Tall brick houses, browbeating each other in gloomy respectability across the white streets; broad pavements, promenaded mainly by the nomadic cat; stifling squares, wherein the infant of unfashionable parentage is taken for the daily baking that is its substitute for the breezes and the press of perambulators on the Bray Esplanade or the Kingstown pier. Few towns are duller out of the season than Dublin, but the dulness of its north side neither waxes nor wanes; it is immutable, unchangeable, fixed as the stars. So at least it appears to the observer whose impressions are only eye-deep, and are derived from the emptiness of the streets, the unvarying dirt of the window panes, and the almost forgotten type of ugliness of the window curtains.

But even an August Sunday in the north side has its distractions for those who know where to seek them, and there are some of a sufficiently ingenuous disposition to find in Sunday-school a social excitement that is independent of fashion, except so far as its slow eddies may have touched the teacher's bonnet. Perhaps it is peculiar to Dublin that Sunday-school, as an institution, is by no means reserved for children of the poorer sort only, but permeates all ranks, and has as many recruits from the upper and middle as from the lower classes. Certainly the excellent Mrs. Fitzpatrick, of Number O, Mountjoy Square, as she lay in mountainous repose on the sofa in her dining-room, had no thought that it was derogatory to the dignity of her daughters and her niece to sit, as they were now sitting, between the children of her grocer, Mr. Mulvany, and her chemist, Mr. Nolan. Sunday-school was, in her mind, an admirable institution that at one and the same time cleared her house of her offspring, and spared her the complications of their religious training, and her broad, black satin-clad bosom rose and fell in rhythmic accord with the snores that were the last expression of Sabbath peace and repose.

It was nearly four o'clock, and the heat and dull clamour in the schoolhouse were beginning to tell equally upon teachers and scholars. Francie Fitzpatrick had yawned twice, though she had a sufficient sense of politeness to conceal the action behind her Bible ; the pleasure of thrusting out in front of her, for the envious regard of her fellows, a new pair of side spring boots, with mock buttons and stitching, had palled upon her ; the spider that had for a few quivering moments hung uncertainly above the gorgeous bonnet of Miss Bewley, the teacher, had drawn itself up again, staggered, no doubt, by the unknown tropic growths it found beneath ; and the silver ring that Tommy Whitty had crammed upon her gloved finger before school, as a mark of devotion, had become perfectly immovable and was a source of at least as much anxiety as satisfaction. Even Miss Bewley's powers of exposition had melted away in the heat ; she had called out her catechetical reserves, and was reduced to a dropping fire of questions as to the meaning of Scriptural names, when at length the superintendent mounted the rostrum and tapped thrice upon it. The closing hymn was sung, and then, class by class, the hot, tired children clattered out into the road.

On Francie rested the responsibilty of bringing home her four small cousins, of ages varying from six to eleven, but this duty did not seem to weigh very heavily on her. She had many acquaintances in the Sunday-school, and with Susie Brennan's and Fanny Hemphill's arms round her waist, and Tommy Whitty in close attendance, she was in no hurry to go home. Children are, if unconsciously, as much influenced by good looks as their elders, and even the raw angularities of fourteen, and Mrs. Fitzpatrick's taste in hats, could not prevent Francie from looking extremely pretty and piquante, as she held forth to an attentive audience on the charms of a young man who had on that day partaken of an early dinner at her Uncle Fitzpatrick's house.

Francie's accent and mode of expressing herself

were alike deplorable ; Dublin had done its worst for her in that respect, but unless the reader has some slight previous notion of how dreadful a thing is a pure-bred Dublin accent, it would be impossible for him to realise in any degree the tone in which she said :

"But oh ! Tommy Whitty ! wait till I tell you what he said about th excursion ! He said he'd come to it if I'd promise to stay with him the whole day ; so now, see how grand I'll be ! And he has a long black mustash ! " she concluded, as a side thrust at Tommy's smooth, apple cheeks.

"Oh, indeed, I'm sure he's a bewty without paint," returned the slighted Tommy, with such sarcasm as he could muster ; "but unless you come in the van with me, the way you said you would, I'll take me ring back from you and give it to Lizzie Jemmison ! So now ! '

"Much I care !" said Francie, tossing her long golden plait of hair, and giving a defiant skip as she walked ; "and what's more, I can't get it off, and nobody will till I die ! and so now yourself !"

Her left hand was dangling over Fanny Hemphill's

shoulder, and she thrust it forward, starfish-wise, in front of Tommy Whitty's face. The silver ring glittered sumptuously on its background of crimson silk glove, and the sudden snatch that her swain made at it was as much impelled by an unworthy desire to repossess the treasure as by the pangs of wounded affection.

"G'long ye dirty fella'!" screamed Francie, in high good-humour, at the same moment eluding the snatch and whirling herself free from the winding embrace of the Misses Hemphill and Brennan; "I dare ye to take it from me!"

She was off like a lapwing down the deserted street, pursued by the more cumbrous Tommy, and by the encouraging yells of the children, who were trooping along the pavement after them. Francie was lithe and swift beyond her fellows, and on ordinary occasions Tommy Whitty, with all his masculine advantage of costume and his two years of seniority, would have found it as much as he could do to catch her. But on this untoward day the traitorous new side spring boots played her false. That decorative band of white stitching across the toes began to press upon her like a vice, and, do what she would, she knew that she could not keep her lead much longer. Strategy was her only resource. Swinging herself round a friendly lamp-post, she stopped short with a suddenness that compelled her pursuer to shoot past her, and with an inspiration whose very daring made it the more delirious, she darted across the street, and sprang into a milk-cart that was waiting at a door. The meek white horse went on at once, and, with a breathless, goading hiss to hasten him, she tried to gather up the reins. Unfortunately, however, it happened that these were under his tail, and the more she tugged at them the tighter he clasped them to him, and the more lively became his trot. In spite of an inexpressible alarm as to the end of the adventure, Francie still retained sufficient presence of mind to put out her tongue at her baffled enemy, as, seated in front of the milk-cans, she clanked past him and the other children. There was a chorus, in tones varying from admiration to horror of, " Oh ! *look* at Francie Fitzpatrick !" and then Tommy Whitty's robuster accents, "Ye'd better look out! the milkman's after ye!"

Francie looked round, and with terror beheld that functionary in enraged pursuit. It was vain to try blandishments with the horse, now making for his stable at a good round trot ; vainer still to pull at the reins. They were nearing the end of the long street, and Francie and the milkman, from their different points of view, were feeling equally help-less and despairing, when a young man came round the corner, and apparently taking in the situation at a glance, ran out into the road, and caught the horse by the bridle.

"Well, upon my word, Miss Francie," he said, as Miss Fitzpatrick hurriedly descended from the cart. "You're a nice young lady ! What on earth are you up to now ? "

"Oh, Mr. Lambert —" began Francie; but having got thus far in her statement, she perceived the justly incensed milkman close upon her, and once more taking to her heels, she left her rescuer to re-turn the stolen property with what explanations he could. Round the corner she fled, and down the next street, till a convenient archway offered a hiding-place, and sheltering there, she laughed, now that the stress of terror was off her, till her blue eyes streamed with tears.

Presently she heard footsteps approaching, and peering cautiously out, saw Lambert striding along with the four Fitzpatrick children dancing round him, in their anxiety to present each a separate version of the escapade. The milkman was not to be seen, and Francie sallied forth to meet the party, secretly somewhat abashed, but resolved to bear an undaunted front before her cousins.

The "long black mustash," so adroitly utilised by Francie for the chastening of Tommy Whitty, was stretched in a wide smile as she looked tentatively at its owner. "Will he tell Aunt Tish?" was the question that possessed her as she entered upon her explanation. The children might be trusted. Their round, white-lashed eyes had witnessed many of her exploits, and their allegiance had never faltered ; but this magnificent grown-up man, who talked to Aunt Tish and Uncle Robert on terms of equality, what trouble might he not get her into in his stupid desire to make a good story of it? "Botheration to him!" she thought, "why couldn't he have been somebody else?"

Mr. Roderick Lambert marched blandly along beside her, with no wish to change places with anyone agitating his bosom. His handsome brown eyes rested approvingly on Francie's flushed face, and the thought that mainly occupied his mind was surprise that Nosey Fitzpatrick should have had such a pretty daughter. He was aware of Francie's diffident glances, but thought they were due to his good looks and his new suit of clothes, and he became even more patronising than before. At last, quite unconsciously, he hit the dreaded point.

" Well, and what do you think your aunt will say when she hears how I found you running away in the milk-cart ? "

" I don't know," replied Francie, getting very red.

"Well, what will you say to me if I don't tell her?"

" Oh, Mr. Lambert, sure you won't tell mamma ! " entreated the Fitzpatrick children, faithful to their leader. " Francie'd be killed if mamma thought she was playing with Tommy Whitty ! "

They were nearing the Fitzpatrick mansion by this time, and Lambert stood still at the foot of the steps and looked down at the small group of petitioners with indulgent self-satisfaction.

"Well, Francie, what'll you do for me if I don't tell?"

Francie walked stiffly up the steps.

"I don't know." Then with a defiance that she was far from feeling, "You may tell her if you like!"

Lambert laughed easily as he followed her up the steps.

"You're very angry with me now, aren't you? Well, never mind, we'll be friends, and I won't tell on you this time."

CHAPTER II.

THE east wind was crying round a small house in the outskirts of an Irish country town. At nightfall it had stolen across the grey expanse of Lough Moyle, and given its first shudder among the hollies and laurestinas that hid the lower windows of Tally Ho Lodge from the too curious passer-by, and at about two o'clock of the November night it was howling so inconsolably in the great tunnel of the kitchen chimney, that Norry the Boat, sitting on a heap of tur by the kitchen fire, drew her shawl closer about her shoulders, and thought gruesomely of the Banshee.

The long trails of the monthly roses tapped and scratched against the window panes, so loudly sometimes that two cats, dozing on the rusty slab of a disused hothearth, opened their eyes and stared, with the expressionless yet wholly alert scrutiny of their race. The objects in the kitchen were scarcely more than visible in the dirty light of a hanging lamp, and the smell of paraffin filled the air. High presses and a dresser lined the walls, and on the top of the dresser, close under the blackened ceiling, it was just possible to make out the ghostly sleeping form of a cockatoo. A door at the end of the kitchen opened into a scullery of the usual prosaic, not to say odorous kind, which was now a cavern of darkness, traversed by twin green stars that moved to and fro as the lights move on a river at night, and looked like anything but what they were, the eyes of cats prowling round a scullery sink.

The tall, yellow-faced cloc gave the gurgle with which it was accustomed to mark the half-hour, and the old woman, as if reminded of her weariness, stretched out her arms and yawned loudly and dismally.

She put back the locks of greyish-red hair that hung over her forehead, and, crouching over the fire-place, she took out of the embers a broken-nosed teapot, and proceeded to pour from it a mug of tea, black with long stewing. She had taken a few sips of it when a bell rang startlingly in the passage outside, jarring the silence of the house with its sharp outcry. Norry the Boat hastily put down her mug, and scrambled to her feet to answer its summons. She groped her way up two cramped flights of stairs that creaked under her as she went, and advanced noiselessly in her stockinged feet across a landing to where a chink of light came from under a door.

The door was opened as she came to it, and a woman's short thick figure appeared in the doorway.

"The mistress wants to see Susan," this person said in a rough whisper ; "is he in the house ? "

" I think he's below in the scullery," returned Norry; "but, my Law ! Miss Charlotte, what does she want of him ?   Is it light in her head she is ? "

" What's that to you ?   Go fetch him at once," replied Miss Charlotte, with a sudden fierceness. She shut the door, and Norry crept downstairs again, making a kind of groaning and lamenting as she went.

Miss Charlotte walked with a heavy step to the fire-place. A lamp was burning dully on a table at the foot of an old-fashioned bed, and the high foot-board threw a shadow that made it difficult to see the occupant of the bed. It was an ordinary little shabby bedroom, the ceiling, seamed with cracks, bulged down till it nearly touched the canopy of the bed. The wall paper had a pattern of blue flowers on a yellowish background ; over the chimney shelf a filmy antique mirror looked strangely refined in the company of the Christmas cards and discoloured photographs that leaned against it. There was no sign of poverty, but everything was dingy, everything was tasteless, from the worn Kidderminster carpet to the illuminated text that was pinned to the wall facing the bed.

Miss Charlotte gave the fire a frugal poke, and lit a candle in the flame provoked from the sulky coals. In doing so some ashes became imbedded in the grease, and taking a hair-pin from the ponderous mass of brown hair that was piled on the back of her head, she began to scrape the candle clean. Probably at no moment of her forty years of life had Miss Charlotte Mullen looked more startlingly plain than now, as she stood, her squat figure draped in a magenta flannel dressing-gown, and the candle light shining upon her face. The night of watching had left its traces upon even her opaque skin. The lines about her prominent mouth and chin were deeper than usual ; her broad cheeks had a flabby pallor ; only her eyes were bright and untired, and the thick yellow-white hand that manipulated the hair-pin was as deft as it was wont to be.

When the flame burned clearly she took the candle to the bedside, and, bending down, held it close to the face of the old woman who was lying there. The eyes opened and turned towards the overhanging face : small dim, blue eyes, full of the stupor of illness, looking out of the pathetically commonplace little old face with a far-away perplexity.

"Was that Francie that was at the door?" she said in a drowsy voice that had in it the lagging drawl of intense weakness.

Charlotte took the tiny wrist in her hand, and felt the pulse with professional attention. Her broad perceptive finger-tips gauged the forces of the little thread that was jerking in the thin network of tendons, and as she laid the hand down she said to herself, "She'll not last out the turn of the night."

"Why doesn't Francie come in ?" murmured the

old woman again in the fragmentary, uninflected voice that seems hardly spared from the unseen battle with death.

. " It wasn't her you asked me for at all," answered Charlotte. " You said you wanted to say good-bye to Susan. Here, you'd better have a sip of this."

The old woman swallowed some brandy and water, and the stimulant presently revived unexpected strength in her.

"Charlotte," she said, " it isn't cats we should be thinking of now. God knows the cats are safe with you. But little Francie, Charlotte, we ought to have done more for her. You promised me that if you got the money you'd look after her. Didn't you now, Charlotte? I wish I'd done more for her. She's a good little thing—a good little thing—" she repeated dreamily.

Few people would think it worth their while to dispute the wandering futilities of an old dying woman, but even at this eleventh hour Charlotte could not brook the revolt of a slave.

"Good little thing !" she exclaimed, pushing the brandy bottle noisily in among a crowd of glasses and medicine bottles, "a strapping big woman of nineteen! You didn't think her so good the time you had her here, and she put Susan's father and mother in the well!"

The old lady did not seem to understand what she had said.

"Susan, Susan!" she called quaveringly, and feebly patted the crochet quilt.

As if in answer, a hand fumbled at the door and opened it softly. Norry was standing there, tall and gaunt, holding in her apron, with both hands, something that looked like an enormous football.

"Miss Charlotte!" she whispered hoarsely, "here's Susan for ye. He was out in the ashpit, an' I was hard set to get him, he was that wild."

Even as she spoke there was a furious struggle in the blue apron.

"God in Heaven! ye fool!" ejaculated Charlotte. "Don't let him go!" She shut the door behind Norry. "Now, give him to me."

Norry opened her apron cautiously, and Miss Charlotte lifted out of it a large grey tom-cat.

"Be quiet, my heart's love," she said, "be quiet."

The cat stopped kicking and writhing, and, sprawling up on to the shoulder of the magenta dressing-gown, turned a fierce grey face upon his late captor. Norry crept over to the bed, and put back the dirty chintz curtain that had been drawn forward to keep out the draught of the door. Mrs. Mullen was lying very still ; she had drawn her knees up in front of her, and the bedclothes hung sharply from the small point that they made. The big living old woman took the hand of the other old woman who was so nearly dead, and pressed her lips to it.

" Ma'am, d'ye know me ? "

Her mistress opened her eyes.

" Norry," she whispered, " give Miss Francie some jam for her tea to-night, but don't tell Miss Charlotte."

" What's that she's saying ? " said Charlotte, going to the other side of the bed. " Is she asking for me ? "

" No, but for Miss Francie," Norry answered.

" She knows as well as I do that Miss Francie's in Dublin," said Charlotte roughly ; " 'twas Susan she was asking for last. Here, a'nt, here's Susan for you."

She pulled the cat down from her shoulder, and put him on the bed, where he crouched with a twitching tail, prepared for flight at a moment's notice.

He was within reach of the old lady's hand, but she did not seem to know that he was there. She opened her eyes and looked vacantly round.

"Where's little Francie? You mustn't send her away, Charlotte; you promised you'd take care of her; didn't you, Charlotte?"

"Yes, yes," said Charlotte quickly, pushing the cat towards the old lady; "never fear, I'll see after her."

Old Mrs. Mullen's eyes, that had rested with a filmy stare on her niece's face, closed again, and her head began to move a little from one side to the other, a low monotonous moan coming from her lips with each turn. Charlotte took her right hand and laid it on the cat's brindled back. It rested there, unconscious, for some seconds, while the two women looked on in silence, and then the fingers drooped and contracted like a bird's claw, and the moaning ceased. There was at the same time a spasmodic movement of the gathered-up knees, and a sudden rigidity fell upon the small insignificant face.

Norry the Boat threw herself upon her knees with a howl, and began to pray loudly. At the sound the cat leaped to the floor, and the hand that had been placed upon him in the only farewell his mistress was to take, dropped stiffly on the bed. Miss Charlotte snatched up the candle, and held it close to her aunt's face. There was no mistaking what she saw there, and, putting down the candle again, she plucked a large silk handkerchief from her pocket, and, with some hideous preliminary heavings of her shoulders, burst into transports of noisy grief.

CHAPTER III.

A DAMP winter and a chilly spring had passed in their usual mildly disagreeable manner over that small Irish country town which was alluded to in the beginning of the last chapter. The shop windows had exhibited their usual zodiacal succession, and had progressed through red comforters and woollen gloves to straw hats, tennis shoes, and coloured Summer Numbers. The residents of Lismoyle were already congratulating each other on having "set" their lodgings to the summer v sitors; the steamer was plying on the lake, the militia was under canvas, and on this very fifteenth of June, Lady Dysart of Bruff was giving her first lawn-tennis party.

Miss Charlotte Mullen had taken advantage of the occasion to emerge from the mourning attire that since her aunt's death had so .misbecome her sallow face, and was driving herself to Bruff in the phæton that had been Mrs. Mullen's, and a gown chosen with rather more view to effect than was customary with her. She was under no delusion as to her appearance, and, early recognising its hopeless character, she had abandoned all superfluities of decoration. A habit of costume so defiantly simple as to border on eccentricity had at least two advantages; it freed her from the absurdity of seeming to admire herself, and it was cheap. During the late Mrs. Mullen's lifetime Charlotte had studied economy. The most reliable old persons had, she was wont to reflect, a slippery turn in them where their wills were concerned, and it was well to be ready for any contingency of fortune. Things had turned out very well after all; there had been one inconvenient legacy—that "Little Francie" to whom the old lady's thoughts had turned, happily too late for her to give any practical emphasis to them—but that bequest was of the kind that may be repudiated if desirable. The rest of the disposition had been admirably convenient, and, in skilled hands, something might even be made of that legacy. Miss Mullen thought

a great deal about her legacy and the steps she
had taken with regard to it as she drove to Bruff.
The horse that drew her ancient phæton moved
with a dignity befitting his eight and twenty years;
the three miles of level lake-side road between
Lismoyle and Bruff were to him a serious under-
taking, and by the time he had arrived at his
destination, his mistress's active mind had pursued
many pleasant mental paths to their utmost limit.

This was the first of the two catholic and
comprehensive entertainments that Lady Dysart's
sense of her duty towards her neighbours yearly
impelled her to give, and when Charlotte, wearing
her company smile, came down the steps of the
terrace to meet her hostess, the difficult revelry
was at its height. Lady Dysart had cast her nets
over a wide expanse, and the result was not
encouraging. She stood, tall, dark, and majestic,
on the terrace, surveying the impracticable row of
women that stretched, forlorn of men, along one
side of the tennis grounds, much as Cassandra
might have scanned the beleaguering hosts from
the ramparts of Troy; and as she advanced to

meet her latest guest, her strong clear-eyed face was perplexed and almost tragic.

"How do you do, Miss Mullen?" she said in tones of unconcealed gloom. "Have you ever seen so few men in your life? and there are five and forty women! I cannot imagine where they have all come from, but I know where I wish they would take themselves to, and that is to the bottom of the lake!"

The large intensity of Lady Dysart's manner gave unintended weight to her most trivial utterance, and had she reflected very deeply before she spoke, it might have occurred to her that this was not a specially fortunate manner of greeting a female guest. But Charlotte understood that nothing personal was intended ; she knew that the freedom of Bruff had been given to her, and that she could afford to listen to abuse of the outer world with the composure of one of the inner circle.

"Well, your ladyship," she said, in the bluff, hearty voice which she felt accorded best with the theory of herself that she had built up in Lady Dysart's mind, "I'll head a forlorn hope to the bottom of the lake for you, and welcome, but for the honour of the house you might give me a cup o' tay first ! "

Charlotte had many tones of voice, according with the many facets of her character, and when she wished to be playful she affected a vigorous brogue, not perhaps being aware that her own accent scarcely admitted of being strengthened.

This refinement of humour was probably wasted on Lady Dysart. She was an Englishwoman, and, as such, was constitutionally unable to discern perfectly the subtle grades of Irish vulgarity. She was aware that many of the ladies on her visiting list were vulgar, but it was their subjects of conversation and their opinions that chiefly brought the fact home to her. Miss Mullen, *au fond*, was probably no less vulgar than they, but she was never dull, and Lady Dysart would suffer anything rather than dulness. It was less than nothing to her that Charlotte's mother was reported to have been in her youth a national schoolmistress, and her grandmother a barefooted country girl. These facts of Miss Mullen's pedigree were valued topics in Lismoyle, but Lady Dysart's serene radicalism ignored the inequalities of a lower class, and she welcomed a woman who could talk to her on spiritualism, or books, or indeed on any current topic, with a point and agreeability that made her accent, to English ears, merely the expression of a vigorous individuality. She now laughed in response to her visitor's jest, but her eye did not cease from roving over the gathering, and her broad brow was still contracted in calculation.

" I never knew the country so bereft of men or so peopled with girls ! Even the little Barrington boys are off with the militia, and everyone about has con-spired to fill their houses with women, and not only women but dummies ! " Her glance lighted on the long bench where sat the more honourable women in midge-bitten dulness. " And there is Kate Gas-cogne in one of her reveries, not hearing a word that Mrs. Waller is saying to her—"

With Lady Dysart intention was accomplishment as nearly as might be. She had scarcely finished speaking before she began a headlong advance upon the objects of her diatribe, making a short cut across the corner of a lawn-tennis court, and scarcely ob-serving the havoc that her transit wrought in the game. Charlotte was less rash. She steered her course clear of the tennis grounds, and of the bench of matrons, passed the six Miss Beatties with a comprehensive " How are ye, girls ? " and took up her position under one of the tall elm trees.

Under the next tree a few·men were assembled, herding together for mutual protection after the manner of men, and laying down the law to each other about road sessions, the grand jury, and Irish politics generally. They were a fairly representative trio ; a country gentleman with a grey moustache and a loud voice in which he was announcing that nothing would give him greater pleasure than to pull the rope at the execution of a certain English states-man ; a slight, dejected-looking clergyman, who vied with Major Waller in his denunciations, but chasten-edly, like an echo in a cathedral aisle ; and a smartly dressed man of about thirty-five, of whom a more detailed description need not be given, as he has been met with in the first chapter, and the six years after nine-and-twenty do little more than mellow a man's taste in checks, and sprinkle a grey hair or two on his temples.

Miss Mullen listened for a few minutes to the melancholy pessimisms of the archdeacon, and then, interrupting Major Waller in a fine outburst on the advisability of martial law, she thrust herself and her attendant cloud of midges into the charmed circle of the smoke of Mr. Lambert's cigarette.

" Ho ! do I hear me old friend the Major at politics ? " she said, shaking hands effusively with the three men. " I declare I'm a better politician than any one of you ! D'ye know how I served Tom Casey, the land-leaguing plumber, yesterday ? I had him mending my tank, and when I got him into it I whipped the ladder away, and told him not a step should he budge till he sang ' God save the Queen ! ' I was arguing there half an hour with him in water up to his middle before I converted him, and then it wasn't so much the warmth of his convictions as the cold of his legs made him tune up. I call that practical politics ! "

The speed and vigour with which this story was told would have astounded anyone who did not know Miss Mullen's powers of narration, but Mr. Lambert, to whom it seemed specially addressed, merely took his cigarette out of his mouth, and said, with a familiar laugh :

"Practical politics, by Jove! I call it a cold water cure. Kill or cure like the rest of your doctoring, eh! Charlotte?"

Miss Mullen joined with entire good-humour in the laugh that followed.

"Oh, th' ingratitude of man!" she exclaimed. "Archdeacon, you've seen his bald scalp from the pulpit, and I ask you, now, isn't that a fresh crop he has on it? I leave it to his conscience, if he has one, to say if it wasn't my doctoring gave him that fine black thatch he has now!"

The archdeacon fixed his eyes seriously upon her ; Charlotte's playfulness always alarmed and confused him.

"Do not appeal to me, Miss Mullen," he answered, in his refined, desponding voice ; "my unfortunate sight makes my evidence in such a matter worth nothing ; and, by the way, I meant to ask you if your niece would be good enough to help us in the choir ? I understand she sings."

Charlotte interrupted him.

"There's another of you at it!" she exclaimed. "I think I'll have to ad*vert*iss it in the *Irish Times* that,' whereas my first cousin, Isabella Mullen, married Johnny Fitzpatrick, who was no relation of mine, good, bad, or indifferent, their child is my first cousin once removed, and *not* my niece!"

Mr. Lambert blew a cloud of smoke through his nose.

"You're a nailer at pedigrees, Charlotte," he said with a patronage that he knew was provoking; "but as far as I can make out the position, it comes to mighty near the same thing; you're what they call her Welsh aunt, anyhow."

Charlotte's face reddened, and she opened her wide mouth for a retort, but before she had time for more than the champings as of a horse with a heavy bit, which preceded her more incisive repartees, another person joined the group.

"Mr. Lambert," said Pamela Dysart, in her pleasant, anxious voice, "I am going to ask you if you will play in the next set, or if you would rather help the Miss Beatties to get up a round of golf? How do you do, Miss Mullen? I have not seen you before ; why did you not bring your niece with you ? ”

Charlotte showed all her teeth in a forced smile as she replied, “I suppose you mean my cousin, Miss Dysart ? she won't be with me till the day after to-morrow.”

“ Oh, I'm so sorry,” replied Pamela, with the sympathetic politeness that made strangers think her manner too good to be true ; “ and Mr. Lambert tells me she plays tennis so well.”

“ Why, what does he know about her tennis playing ? ” said Charlotte, turning sharply towards Lambert.

The set on the nearer court was over, and the two young men who had played in it strolled up to the group as she spoke. Mr. Lambert expanded his broad chest, gave his hat an extra tilt over his nose, and looked rather more self-complacent than usual as he replied :

“ Well, I ought to know something about it, seeing I took her in hand when she was in short petticoats—taught her her paces myself, in fact.”

Mr. Hawkins, the shorter of the two players who

had just come up, ceased from mopping his scarlet face, and glanced from Mr. Lambert to Pamela with a countenance devoid of expression, save that conferred by the elevation of one eyebrow almost to the roots of his yellow hair. Pamela's eyes remained unresponsive, but the precipitancy with which she again addressed herself to Mr. Lambert showed that a disposition to laugh had been near.

Charlotte turned away with an expression that was the reverse of attractive. When her servants saw that look they abandoned excuse or discussion; when the Lismoyle beggars saw it they checked the flow of benediction and fled. Even the archdeacon, through the religious halo that habitually intervened between him and society, became aware that the moment was not propitious for speaking to Miss Mullen about his proposed changes in the choir, and he drifted away to think of diocesan matters, and to forget as far as possible that he was at a lawn-tennis party.

Outside the group stood the young man who had been playing in the set with Mr. Hawkins. He was watching through an eyeglass the limp progress of the game in the other court, and was even making praiseworthy attempts to applaud the very feeble efforts of the players. He was tall and slight, with a near-sighted stoop, and something of an old-fashioned, eighteenth century look about him that was accentuated by his not wearing a moustache, and was out of keeping with the flannels and brilliant blazer that are the revolutionary protest of this age against its orthodox clothing. It did not seem to occur to him that he was doing anything unusual in occupying himself, as he was now doing, in picking up balls for the Lismoyle curate and his partner ; he would have thought it much more remarkable had he found in himself a preference for doing anything else. This was an occupation that demanded neither interest nor conversation, and of a number of disagreeable duties he did not think that he had chosen the worst.

Charlotte walked up to him as he stood leaning against a tree, and held out her hand.

" How d'ye do, Mr. Dysart ? " she said with marked politeness. All trace of combat had left her manner, and the smile with which she greeted him was sweet and capacious. " We haven't seen you in

Lismoyle since you came back from the West Indies."

Christopher Dysart let his eyeglass fall, and looked apologetic as he enclosed her well-filled glove in his long hand, and made what excuses he could for not having called upon Miss Mullen.

"Since Captain Thesiger has got this new steam-launch I can't call my soul my own; I'm out on the lake with him half the day, and the other half I spend with a nail-brush trying to get the blacks off."

He spoke with a hesitation that could hardly be called a stammer, but was rather a delaying before his sentences, a mental rather than a physical un-certainty.

"Oh, that's a very poor excuse," said Charlotte with loud affability, "deserting your old friends for the blacks a second time! I thought you had enough of them in the last two years! And you know you promised—or your good mother did for you—that you'd come and photograph poor old Mrs. Tommy before she died. The poor thing's so sick now we have to feed her with a baby's bottle."

Christopher wondered if Mrs. Tommy were the

cook, and was on the point of asking for further particulars, when Miss Mullen continued:

" She's the great-great-grandmother of all me cats, and I want you to immortalise her; but don't come till after Monday, as I'd like to introduce you to my cousin, Miss Fitzpatrick; did you hear she was coming ? "

" Yes, Mr. Lambert told us she was to be here next week," said Christopher, with an indescribable expression that was not quite amusement, but was something more than intelligence.

" What did he say of her ? "

Christopher hesitated ; somehow what he remembered of Mr. Lambert's conversation was of too free and easy a nature for repetition to Miss Fitzpatrick's cousin.

" He—er—seemed to think her very—er—charming in all ways," he said rather lamely.

" So it's talking of charming young ladies you and Roddy Lambert are when he comes to see you on estate business ! " said Charlotte archly, but with a rasp in her voice. " When my poor father was your father's agent, and I used to be helping him in the office, it was charming young cattle we talked about, and not young ladies."

Christopher laughed in a helpless way.

" I wish you were at the office still, Miss Mullen ; if anyone could understand the Land Act I believe it would be you."

At this moment there was an upheaval among the matrons ; the long line rose and broke, and made for the grey stone house whose windows were flashing back the sunlight through the trees at the end of the lawn-tennis grounds. The tedious skirmish with midges, and the strain of inactivity were alike over for the present, and the conscience of the son of the house reminded him that he ought to take Miss Mullen in to tea.

CHAPTER IV.

THERE was consternation among the cats at Tally Ho Lodge; a consternation mingled with righteous resentment. Even the patriarchal Susan could scarcely remember the time that the spare bedroom had been anything else than an hospital, a nursery, and a secure parliament house for him and his descendants; yet now, in his old age, and when he had, after vast consideration of alternatives, allocated to himself the lowest shelf of the wardrobe as a sleeping place, he was evicted at a moment's notice, and the folded-away bed curtains that had formed his couch were even now perfuming the ambient air as they hung out of the window over the hall door. Susan was too dignified to give utterance to his wounded feelings; he went away by himself, and, sitting on the roof of the fowl-house, thought unutterable things. But his great-niece, Mrs. Bruff, could

not emulate his stoicism. Followed by her five latest
kittens, she strode through the house, uttering harsh
cries of rage and despair, and did not cease from her
lamentations until Charlotte brought the whole party
into the drawing-room, and established them in the
waste-paper basket.

The worst part about the upheaval, as even the
youngest and least experienced of the cats could see,
was that it was irrevocable. It was early morning
when the first dull blow of Norry's broom against the
wainscot had startled them with new and strange ap-
prehension, and incredulity had grown to certainty,
till the final moment when the sight of a brimming
pail of water urged them to panic-struck flight. It
may be admitted that Norry the Boat, who had not,
as a rule, any special taste for cleanliness, had seldom
enjoyed anything more than this day of turmoil, this
routing of her ancient enemies. Miss Charlotte, to
whom on ordinary occasions the offended cat never
appealed in vain, was now bound by her own word.
She had given orders that the spare room was to be
" cleaned down," and cleaned down it surely should be.
It was not, strictly speaking, Norry's work. Louisa

was house and parlour-maid ; Louisa, a small and sullen Protestant orphan of unequalled sluggishness and stupidity, for whose capacity for dealing with any emergency Norry had a scorn too deep for any words that might conveniently be repeated here. It was not likely that Louisa would be permitted to join in the ardours of the campaign, when even Bid Sal, Norry's own special kitchen-slut and co-religionist, was not allowed to assist.

Norry the Boat, daughter of Shaunapickeen, the ferryman (whence her title), and of Carroty Peg his wife, was a person with whom few would have cared to co-operate against her will. On this morning she wore a more ferocious aspect that usual. Her roughly-waving hair, which had never known the dignity of a cap, was bound up in a blue duster, leaving her bony forehead bare ; dust and turf-ashes hung in her grizzled eyebrows, her arms were smeared with blacklead, and the skirt of her dress was girt about her waist, displaying a petticoat of heavy Galway flannel, long thin legs, and enormous feet cased in countrymen's laced boots. It was fifteen years now, Norry reflected, while she scrubbed the floor and scraped the candle drippings off it with her nails, since Miss Charlotte and the cats had come into . the house, and since then the spare room had never • had a visitor into it. Nobody had stayed in the house in all those years except little Miss Francie, and for her the cot had been made up in her great-aunt's room ; the old high-sided cot in which her grandmother had slept when she was a child. The cot had long since migrated into the spare room, and from it Norry had just ejected the household effects of Mrs. Bruff and her family, with a pleasure that was mitigated only by the thought that Miss Francie was a young woman now, and would be likely to give a good deal more trouble in the house than even in the days when she stole the cockatoo's sopped toast for her private consumption, and christened the tom-cat Susan against everyone's wishes except her great-aunt's.

Norry and the cockatoo were now the only sur-vivors of the old *régime* at Tally Ho Lodge, in fact the cockatoo was regarded in Lismoyle as an almost prehistoric relic, dating, at the lowest computation, from the days when old Mrs. Mullen's fox-hunting

father had lived there, and given the place the name
that was so remarkably unsuited to its subsequent
career.   The cockatoo was a sprightly creature of
some twenty shrieking summers on the day that the
two Miss Butlers, clad in high-waisted, low-necked
gowns, were armed past his perch in the hall by their
father, and before, as it seemed to the cockatoo, he
had more than half-finished his morning dose, they
were back again, this time on the arms of the two
young men who, during the previous five months, had
done so much to spoil his digestion by propitiatory
dainties at improper hours.   The cockatoo had no
very clear recollection of the subsequent departure of
Dr. Mullen and his brother, the attorney, with their
brides, on their respective honeymoons, owing to the
fact that Mr. Mullen, the agent, brother of the two
bridegrooms, had prised open his beak, and compelled
him to drink the healths of the happy couples in the
strongest and sweetest whisky punch.

The cockatoo's memory after this climax was filled
with vague comings and goings, extending over unknown tracts of time.   He remembered two days of
disturbance, on each of which a long box had been

carried out of the house by several men, and a crowd of people, dressed in black, had eaten a long and clattering meal in the dining-room. He had always remembered the second of these occasions with just annoyance, because, in manœuvring the long box through the narrow hall, he had been knocked off his perch, and never after that day had the person whom he had been taught to call " Doctor " come to give him his daily lump of sugar.

But the day that enunciated itself most stridently from the cockatoo's past life was that on which the doctor's niece had, after many short visits, finally arrived with several trunks, and a wooden case from which, when opened, sprang four of the noisome creatures whom Miss Charlotte, their owner, had taught him to call " pussies." A long era of persecution then began for him, of robbery of his food, and even attacks upon his person. He had retaliated by untiring mimicry, by delusive invitations to food in the manner of Miss Charlotte, and lastly, by the strangling of a too-confiding kitten, whom he had lured, with maternal mewings, within reach of his claws. That very day Miss Charlotte's hand avenged the murder, and afterwards conveyed him, a stiff guilty lump of white feathers, to the top of the kitchen press, from thenceforth never to descend, except when long and patient picking had opened a link of his chain, or when, on fine days, Norry fastened him to a branch of the tall laurel that overhung the pig-stye. Norry was his only friend, a friendship slowly cemented by a common hatred of the cats and Louisa ; indeed, it is probable that but for occasional conversation with Norry he would have choked from his own misanthropic fury, helpless, lonely spectator as he was of the secret gluttonies of Louisa, and the maddening domestic felicity of the cats.

But on this last day of turbulence and rout he had been forgotten. The kitchen was sunny and stuffy, the bluebottles were buzzing their loudest in the cobwebby window, one colony of evicted kittens was already beginning to make the best of things in the turf heap, and the leaves of the laurel outside were gleaming tropically against the brilliant sky, with no one to appreciate them except the pigs. When it came to half-past twelve o'clock the cockatoo could no longer refrain, and fell to loud and prolonged screamings. The only result at first was a brief stupefaction on the part of the kittens, and an answering outcry from the fowl in the yard; then, after some minutes, the green baize cross-door opened, and a voice bellowed down the passage:

"Biddy! Bid Sal!" (*fortissimo*), "can't ye stop that bird's infernal screeching?" There was dead silence, and Miss Mullen advanced into the kitchen and called again.

"Biddy's claning herself, Miss Mullen," said a small voice from the pantry door.

"That's no reason you shouldn't answer!" thundered Charlotte; "come out here yourself and put the cockatoo out in the yard."

Louisa, the orphan, a short, fat, white-faced girl of fourteen, shuffled out of the pantry with her chin buried in her chest, and her round terrified eyes turned upwards to Miss Charlotte's face.

"I'd be in dhread to ketch him," she faltered.

Those ladies who considered Miss Mullen "eccentric, but so kind-hearted, and so clever and agreeable," would have been considerably surprised if they had heard the terms in which she informed Louisa that she was wanting in courage and intelligence ; but Louisa's face expressed no surprise, only a vacancy that in some degree justified her mistress's language. Still denouncing her retainers, Miss Charlotte mounted nimbly upon a chair, and seizing the now speechless cockatoo by the wings, carried him herself out to the yard and fastened him to his accustomed laurel bough.

She did not go back to the kitchen, but, after a searching glance at the contents of the pigs' trough, went out of the yard by the gate that led to the front of the house. Rhododendrons and laurels made a dark green tunnel about her, and, though it was June, the beech leaves of last November lay rotting on each side of the walk. Opposite the hall door the ground rose in a slight slope, thickly covered with evergreens, and topped by a lime tree, on whose lower limbs a flock of black turkeys had ranged themselves in sepulchral meditation. The house itself was half stifled with ivy, monthly roses, and virginian creeper ; everywhere was the same un-kempt profusion of green things, that sucked the sunshine into themselves, and left the air damp and shadowed. Charlotte had the air of thinking very deeply as she walked slowly along with her hands in the pockets of her black alpaca apron. The wrinkles on her forehead almost touched the hair that grew so low down upon it as to seem like a wig that had been pulled too far over the turn of the brow, and she kept chewing at her heavy underlip as was her habit during the processes of unobserved thought. Then she went into the house, and, sitting down at the davenport in the dining-room, got out a sheet of her best notepaper, and wrote a note to Pamela Dysart in her strong, commercially clear hand.

Afternoon tea had never flourished as an institution at Tally Ho Lodge. Occasionally, and of necessity, a laboured repast had been served at five o'clock by the trembling Louisa ; occasions on which the afternoon caller had not only to suffer the spectacle of a household being shaken to its foundations on her behalf, but had subsequently to eat of the untempting fruit of these struggles. On the afternoon, however, of the day following that of the cleansing of the spare room, timely preparations had been made. Half the round table in the centre of the drawing-room had been covered with a cloth, and on it Louisa, in the plenitude of her zeal, had prepared a miniature breakfast ; loaf, butter-cooler, and knives and forks, a truly realistic touch being conferred by two egg - cups standing in the slop-basin. A vase of marigolds and pink sweet pea stood behind these, a fresh heap of shavings adorned the grate, the piano had been opened and dusted, and a copy of the " Indiana Waltzes " frisked on the desk in the breeze from the open window.

Charlotte sat in a low armchair and surveyed her drawing-room with a good deal of satisfaction. Her fingers moved gently through the long fur at the back of Mrs. Bruff's head, administering, almost unconsciously, the most delicately satisfactory scratching about the base of the wide, sensitive ears, while her eyes wandered back to the pages of the novel that lay open on her lap. She was a great and insatiable reader, surprisingly well acquainted with the classics of literature, and unexpectedly lavish in the purchase of books. Her neighbours never forgot to mention, in describing her, the awe-inspiring fact that she "took in the *English Times* and the *Saturday*

Review, and read every word of them," but it was hinted that the bookshelves that her own capable hands had put up in her bedroom held a large proportion of works of fiction of a startlingly advanced kind, " and," it was generally added in tones of mystery, " many of them French."

It was half-past five o'clock, and the sharpest of several showers that had fallen that day had caused Miss Mullen to get up and shut the window, when the grinding of the gate upon the gravel at the end of the short drive warned her that the expected guest was arriving. As she got to the hall door one of those black leather band-boxes on wheels, known in the south and west of Ireland as " jingles " or inside cars, came brushing under the arch of wet evergreens, and she ran out on to the steps.

" Well, my dear child, welcome to Tally Ho ! " she began in tones of effusive welcome, as the car turned and backed towards the doorstep in the accustomed way, then seeing through the half-closed curtains that there was nothing inside it except a trunk and a bonnet box, " Where in the name of goodness is the young lady, Jerry?   Didn't you meet her at the train?"

" I did to be sure," replied Jerry; "sure she's afther me on the road now. Mr. Lambert came down on the thrain with her, and he's dhrivin' her here in his own thrap."

While he was speaking there was the sound of quick trotting on the road, and Miss Mullen saw a white straw hat and a brown billycock moving swiftly along over the tops of the evergreens. A dog-cart with a white-faced chestnut swung in at the gate, and Miss Fitzpatrick's hat was immediately swept off her head by a bough of laburnum. Its owner gave a shrill cry and made a snatch at the reins, with the idea apparently of stopping the horse.

" No, you don't," said Mr. Lambert, intercepting the snatch with his whip hand; "you're going to be handed over to your aunt just as you are."

Half a dozen steps brought them to the door, and the chestnut pulled up with his pink nose almost between the curtains of the inside car. It was hard to say whether Miss Mullen had heard Lambert's remark, which had certainly been loud enough to enable her to do so, but her only reply was an attack upon the carman.

"Take your car out o' that, ye great oaf!" she vociferated; "can't ye make way for your betters?" Then with a complete change of voice, "Well, me dear Francie, you're welcome, you're welcome."

The greeting was perceptibly less hearty than that which had been squandered on the trunk and bonnet box; but an emotion *réchauffé* necessarily loses flavour. Francie had jumped to the ground with a reckless disregard of the caution demanded by the steps of a dog-cart, and stooping her hatless head, kissed the hard cheek that Charlotte tendered for her embrace.

"Thank you very much, I'm very glad to come," she said, in a voice whose Dublin accent had been but little modified by the six years that had lightly gone over her since the August Sunday when she had fled from Tommy Whitty in the milkman's cart. "And look at me the show I am without my hat! And it's all his fault!" with a lift of her blue eyes to Lambert, "he wouldn't let me stop and pick it up."

Charlotte looked up at her with the wide smile of welcome still stiff upon her face. The rough golden heap of curls on the top of Francie's head was spangled with raindrops and her coat was grey with wet.

"Well, if Mr. Lambert had had any sense," said Miss Mullen, "he'd have let you come in the covered car. Here, Louisa, go fetch Miss Fitzpatrick's hat."

"Ah, no, sure she'll get all wet," said Francie, starting herself before the less agile Louisa could emerge from behind her mistress, and running down the drive.

"Did you come down from Dublin to-day, Roddy?" said Charlotte.

"Yes, I did," answered Mr. Lambert, turning his horse as he spoke; "I had business that took me up to town yesterday, so it just happened that I hit off Francie. Well, good evening. I expect Lucy will be calling round to see you to-morrow or next day."

He walked his horse down the drive, and as he passed Francie returning with her hat he leaned over the wheel and said something to her that made her shake her head and laugh. Miss Charlotte was too far off to hear what it was.

CHAPTER V.

IT was generally felt in Lismoyle that Mr. Roderick Lambert held an unassailable position in society. The Dysart agency had always been considered to confer brevet rank as a country gentleman upon its owner, apart even from the intimacy with the Dysarts which it implied ; and as, in addition to these advantages, Mr. Lambert possessed good looks, a wife with money, and a new house at least a mile from the town, built under his own directions and at his employer's expense, Lismoyle placed him un-hesitatingly at the head of its visiting list. Of course his wife was placed there too, but somehow or other Mrs. Lambert was a person of far less con-sequence than her husband. She had had the money certainly, but that quality was a good deal over-looked by the Lismoyle people in their admiration for the manner in which her husband spent it. It

was natural that they should respect the captor
rather than the captive, and, in any case, Mr.
Roderick Lambert's horses and traps were more im-
pressive facts than the Maltese terrier and the shelf
of patent medicines that were Mrs. Lambert's only
extravagances.

Possibly, also, the fact that she had no children
placed her at a disadvantage with the matrons of
Lismoyle, all of whom could have spoken fearlessly
with their enemies in the gate ; it deprived conversation with her of the antiphonal quality, when
mother answers unto mother of vaccination and
teething-rash, and the sins of the nursery-maids are
visited upon the company generally.

" Ah, she's a poor peenie-weenie thing ! " said Mrs.
Baker, who was usually the mouth-piece of Lismoyle
opinion, " and it's no wonder that Lambert's for ever
flourishing about the country in his dog-trap, and she
never seeing a sight of him from morning till night.
I'd like to see Mr. Baker getting up on a horse and
galloping around the roads after bank hours, instead of coming in for his cup of tea with me and the
girls ! "

Altogether the feeling was that Mrs. Lambert was a failure, and in spite of her undoubted amiability, and the creditable fact that Mr. Lambert was the second husband that the eight thousand pounds ground out by her late father's mills had procured for her, her spouse was regarded with a certain regretful pity as the victim of circumstance.

In spite of his claims upon the sympathy of Lismoyle, Mr. Lambert looked remarkably well able to compete with his lot in life, as he sat smoking his pipe in his dinner costume of carpet slippers and oldest shooting coat, a couple of evenings after Francie's arrival. As a rule the Lamberts preferred to sit in their dining-room. The hard magnificence of the blue rep chairs in the drawing-room appealed to them from different points of view; Mrs. Lambert holding that they were too good to be used except by " company," while Mr. Lambert truly felt that no one who was not debarred by politeness from the power of complaint would voluntarily sit upon them. An unshaded lamp was on the table, its ugly glare conflicting with the soft remnants of June twilight that stole in between the half-drawn curtains ; a

tumbler of whisky and water stood on the corner of
the table beside the comfortable leather-covered
armchair in which the master of the house was read-
ing his paper, while opposite to him, in a basket
chair, his wife was conscientiously doing her fancy
work.   She was a short woman with confused brown
eyes and distressingly sloping shoulders ; a woman
of the turkey hen type, dejected and timorous in
voice, and an habitual wearer of porous plasters.
Her toilet for the evening consisted in replacing by
a white cashmere shawl the red knitted one which
she habitually wore, and a languid untidyness in the
pale brown hair that hung over her eyes intimated
that she had tried to curl her fringe for dinner.

Neither were speaking ; it seemed as if Mr. Lambert were placidly awaiting the arrival of his usual
after-dinner sleep ; the Maltese terrier was already
snoring plethorically on his mistress's lap, in a
manner quite disproportioned to his size, and Mrs.
Lambert's crochet needles were moving more and
more slowly through the mazes of the "bosom
friend" that she was making for herself, the knowledge that the minute hand of the black marble clock

was approaching the hour at which she took her post-prandial pill alone keeping her from also yielding to the soft, influences of a substantial meal. At length she took the box from the little table beside her, where it stood between a bottle of smelling-salts and a lump of camphor, and having sat with it in her hand till the half hour was solemnly boomed from the chimney-piece, swallowed her pill with practised ease. At the slight noise of replacing the box her husband opened his eyes.

"By the way, Lucy," he said in a voice that had no trace of drowsiness in it, "did Charlotte Mullen say what she was going to do to-morrow?"

"Oh, yes, Roderick," replied Mrs. Lambert a little anxiously, "indeed, I was wanting to tell you— Charlotte asked me if I could drive her over to Mrs. Waller's to-morrow afternoon. I forgot to ask you before if you wanted the horses."

Mr. Lambert's fine complexion deepened by one or two shades.

"Upon my soul, Charlotte Mullen has a good cheek! She gets as much work out of my horses as I do myself. I suppose you told her you'd do it?"

"Well, what else could I do?" replied Mrs. Lambert with tremulous crossness; "I'm sure it's not once in the month I get outside the place, and, as for Charlotte, she has not been to the Waller's since before Christmas, and you know very well old Captain couldn't draw her eight miles there and eight miles back any more than the cat."

"Cat be hanged! Why the devil can't she put her hand in her pocket and take a car for herself?" said Lambert, uncrossing his legs and sitting up straight; "I suppose I'll hear next that I'm not to order out my own horses till I've sent round to Miss Mullen to know if she wants them first! If you weren't so infernally under her thumb you'd remember there were others to be consulted besides her."

"I'm not under her thumb, Roderick; I'll beg you'll not say such a thing," replied Mrs. Lambert huffily, her eyes blinking with resentment. "Charlotte Mullen's an old friend of mine, and yours too, and it's a hard thing I can't take her out driving without remarks being passed, and I never thought you'd want the horses. I thought you said you'd be in the office all to-morrow," ended the poor turkey hen, whose feathers were constitutionally incapable of remaining erect for any length of time.

Lambert did not answer immediately. His eyes rested on her flushed face with just enough expression in them to convey to her that her protest was beside the point. Mrs. Lambert was apparently used to this silent comment on what she said, for she went on still more apologetically :

"If you like, Roderick, I'll send Michael over early with a note to Charlotte to tell her we'll go some other day."

Mr. Lambert leaned back as if to consider the question, and began to fill his pipe for the second time.

"Well," he said slowly, "if it makes no difference to you, Lucy, I'd be rather glad if you did. As a matter of fact I have to ride out to Gurthnamuckla to-morrow, on business, and I thought I'd take Francie Fitzpatrick with me there on the black mare. She's no great shakes of a rider, and the black mare is the only thing I'd like to put her on. But, of course, if it was for your own sake and not Charlotte's that you wanted to go to the Waller's, I'd try and manage to take Francie some other day. For the matter of that I might put her on Paddy ; I daresay he'd carry a lady."

Mr. Lambert's concession had precisely the expected effect. Mrs. Lambert gave a cry of consternation :

" Roderick ! you wouldn't ! Is it put that girl up on that mad little savage of a pony ! Why, it's only yesterday, when Michael was driving me into town, and Mr. Corkran passed on his tricycle, he tore up on to his hind heels and tried to run into Ryan's public house ! Indeed, if that was the way, not all the Charlottes in the world would make me go driving to-morrow."

"Oh, all right," said Lambert graciously ; " if you'd rather have it that way, we'll send a note over to Charlotte."

" Would you mind—" said Mrs. Lambert hesitatingly. " I mean, don't you think it would be better if—supposing you wrote the note ? She always minds what you say, and, I declare, I don't know how in the world I'd make up the excuse, when she'd settled the whole thing, and even got me to leave word with the sweep to do her drawing-room chimney that's thick with jackdaws' nests, because the family'd be from home all the afternoon."

"Why, what was to happen to Francie?" asked Lambert quickly.

"I think Charlotte said she was to come with us," yawned Mrs. Lambert, whose memory for conversation was as feeble as the part she played in it; "they had some talk about it at all events. I wouldn't be sure but Francie Fitzpatrick said first she'd go for a walk to see the town—yes, so she did, and Charlotte told her what she was going for was to try and see the officers, and Francie said maybe it was, or maybe she'd come and have afternoon tea with you. They had great joking about it, but I'm sure, after all, it was settled she was to come with us. Indeed," continued Mrs. Lambert meditatively; "I think Charlotte's quite right not to have her going through the town that way by herself; for, I declare, Roderick, that's a lovely girl."

"Oh, she's well able to take care of herself," said Lambert, with the gruff deprecation that is with some people the method of showing pleasure at a compliment. "She's not such a fool as she looks, I can tell you," he went on, feeling suddenly quite companionable ; "the Fitzpatricks didn't take such wonderful care of her that Charlotte need be bothering herself to put her in cotton wool at this time of day."

Mrs. Lambert crocheted on in silence for a few moments, inwardly counting her stitches till she came to the end of the row, then she withdrew the needle and scratched her head ruminatingly with it.

"Isn't it a strange thing, Roderick, what makes Charlotte have anyone staying in the house with her? I never remember such a thing to happen before."

"She has to have her, and no thanks to her. Old Fitzpatrick's been doing bad business lately, and the little house he's had to take at Bray is a tight fit for themselves and the children; so, as he said to me, he thought it was time for Charlotte to do something for her own cousin's child, and no such great thanks to her either, seeing she got every halfpenny the old woman had."

Mrs. Lambert realised that she was actually carrying on a conversation with her husband, and nervously cast about in her mind for some response that should be both striking and stimulating.

"Well, now, if you want my opinion," she said, shutting both her eyes and shaking her head with the peculiar arch sagacity of a dull woman, "I wouldn't be surprised if Charlotte wasn't so sorry to have her here after all. Maybe she thinks she might snap up one of the officers—or there's young Charley Flood—or, Roderick!" Mrs. Lambert almost giggled with delight and excitement—"I wouldn't put it past Charlotte to be trying to ketch Mr. Dysart."

Roderick laughed in a disagreeable way.

"I'd wish her joy of him if she got him! A fellow that'd rather stick at home there at Bruff having tea with his sister than go down like any other fellow and play a game of pool at the hotel! A sort of chap that says, if you offer him a whisky and soda in a friendly way, 'Th—thanks—I don't c—care about anything at this t—t—time of day.' I think Francie'd make him sit up!" Mr. Lambert felt his imitation of Christopher Dysart's voice to be a

success, and the shrill burst of laughter with which
Mrs. Lambert greeted it gave him for the moment an
unusual tinge of respect for her intelligence. "That's
about the size of it, Lucy, what?"

"Oh, Roderick, how comical you are!" responded
the dutiful turkey hen, wiping her watery eyes; "it
reminds me of the days when you used to be talking
of old Mr. Mullen and Charlotte fighting in the office
till I'd think I was listening to themselves."

"God help the man that's got to fight with Charlotte, anyhow!" said Lambert, finishing his whisky
and water as if toasting the sentiment; "and talking
of Charlotte, Lucy, you needn't mind about writing
that note to her; I'll go over myself and speak to
her in the morning."

"Oh, yes, Roderick, 'twill be all right if you see
herself, and you might say to her that I'll be expect-
ing her to come in to tea."

Mr. Lambert, who had already taken up his
newspaper again, merely grunted an assent. Mrs.
Lambert patiently folded her small bony hands upon
her dog's back, and closing her eyes and opening her
mouth, fell asleep in half a dozen breaths.

Her husband read his paper for a short time, while the subdued duet of snoring came continuously from the chair opposite. The clock struck nine in its sonorous, gentlemanlike voice, and at the sound Lambert threw down his paper as if an idea had occurred to him. He got up and went over to the window, and putting aside the curtains, looked out into the twilight of the June evening. The world outside was still awake, and the air was tender with the remembrance of the long day of sunshine and heat; a thrush was singing loudly down by the seringa bush at the end of the garden; the cattle were browsing and breathing audibly in the field beyond, and some children were laughing and shouting on the road. It seemed to Lambert much earlier than he had thought, and as he stood there, the invitation of the summer evening began to appeal to him with seductive force; the quiet fields lay grey and mysterious under the pale western glow, and his eye travelled several times across them to a distant dark blot—the clump of trees and evergreens in which Tally Ho Lodge lay buried.

He turned from the window at last, and coming

back into the lamplit room, surveyed it and its unconscious occupants with a feeling of intolerance for
their unlovely slumber. His next step was the
almost unprecedented one of changing his slippers for
boots, and in a few minutes he had left the house.

CHAPTER VI.

NORRY THE BOAT toiled up the back stairs with wrath in her heart. She had been listening for some minutes with grim enjoyment to cries from the landing upstairs; unavailing calls for Louisa, interspersed with the dumb galvanic quiver of a bell-less bellwire, and at last Francie's voice at the angle half-way down the kitchen stairs had entreated her to find and despatch to her the missing Protestant orphan. Then Norry had said to herself, while she lifted the pot of potatoes off the fire, " Throuble-the-house! God knows I'm heart-scalded with the whole o' yees!" And then aloud, " She's afther goin' out to the dhryin' ground to throw out a few aper'rns to blaych."

"Well, I *must* have somebody; I can't get my habit on," the voice had wailed in reply. " Couldn't you come, Norry?"

As we have said, Norry ascended the stairs with wrath in her heart, as gruesome a lady's-maid as could well be imagined, with an apron mottled with grease spots, and a stale smell of raw onions pervading her generally. Francie was standing in front of the dim looking-glass with which Charlotte chastened the vanity of her guests, trying with stiff and tired fingers to drag the buttons of a brand new habit through the unyielding buttonholes that tailors alone have the gift of making, and Norry's anger was forgotten in prayerful horror, as her eyes wandered from the hard felt hat to the trousered ankle that appeared beneath the skimpy and angular skirt.

"The Lord look down in pity on thim that cut that petticoat!" she said. "Sure, it's not out in the sthreets ye're goin' in the like o' that! God knows it'd be as good. for ye to be dhressed like a man altogether!"

"I wouldn't care what I was dressed like if I could only make the beastly thing meet," said Francie, her face flushed with heat and effort; "wasn't I the fool to tell him to make it tight in the waist!"

The subsequent proceedings were strenuous, but in

the end successful, and finally Miss Fitzpatrick walked stiffly downstairs, looking very slender and tall, with the tail of the dark green habit—she had felt green to be the colour consecrated to sport— drawn tightly round her, and a silver horse-shoe brooch at her throat.

Charlotte was standing at the open hall door talking to Mr. Lambert.

" Come along, child," she said genially, " you've been so long adorning yourself that nothing but his natural respect for the presence of a lady kept this gentleman from indulging in abusive language."

Charlotte, in her lighter moods, was addicted to a ponderous persiflage, the aristocratic foster-sister of her broader peasant jestings in the manner of those whom she was fond of describing as " the bar purple."

Mr. Lambert did not trouble himself to reply to this sally. He was looking at the figure in the olive-green habit, that was advancing along the path of sunlight to the doorway, and thinking that he had done well to write that letter on the subject of the riding that Francie might expect to have at

Lismoyle.   Charlotte turned her head also to look at the radiant, sunlit figure.

"Why, child, were you calling Norry just now to melt you down and pour you into that garment?   I never saw such a waist!   Take care and don't let her fall off, Roddy, or she'll snap in two!"   She laughed loudly and discordantly, looking to Mr. Lambert's groom for the appreciation that was lacking in the face of his master; and during the arduous process of getting Miss Fitzpatrick into her saddle she remained on the steps, offering facetious suggestions and warnings, with her short arms akimbo, and a smile that was meant to be jovial accentuating the hard lines of her face.

At last the green habit was adjusted, the reins placed properly between Francie's awkward fingers, and Mr. Lambert had mounted his long-legged young chestnut and was ready to start.

"Don't forget Lucy expects you to tea, Charlotte," he said as he settled himself in his saddle.

"And don't you forget what I told you," replied Charlotte, sinking her voice confidentially; "don't mind her if she opens her mouth wide, it'll take less to shut it than ye'd think."

Lambert nodded and rode after Francie, who, in compliance with the wishes of the black mare, had hurried on towards the gate. The black mare was a lady of character, well-mannered but firm, and the mere sit of the saddle on her back told her that this was a case when it would be well to take matters into her own control; she accordingly dragged as much of the reins as she required from Francie's helpless hands, and by the time she had got on to the high road had given her rider to understand that her position was that of tenant at will.

They turned their backs on the town, and rode along the dazzling, dusty road, that radiated all the heat of a blazing afternoon.

"I think he did you pretty well with that habit," remarked Lambert presently. "What's the damage to be?"

"What do you think?" replied Francie gaily, answering one question with another after the manner of her country.

"Ten?"

"Ah, go on! Where'd I get ten pounds? He said he'd only charge me six because you recommended me, but I can tell him he'll have to wait for his money."

" Why, are you hard up again ? "

Francie looked up at him and laughed with unconcern that was not in the least affected.

" Of course I am ! Did you ever know me that I wasn't ? "

Lambert was silent for a moment or two, and half unconsciously his thoughts ran back over the time, six years ago now, when he had first met Francie. There had always been something exasperating to him in her brilliant indifference to the serious things of life. Her high spirits were as impenetrable as a coat of mail; her ignorance of the world was at once sublime and enraging. She had not seemed in the least impressed by the fact that he, whom up to this time she had known as merely a visitor at her uncle's house, a feature of the Lawn-Tennis tournament week, and a person with whom to promenade Merrion Square while the band was playing, was, in reality, a country gentleman, a J.P., and a man of standing, who owned as good horses as anyone in the country. She even seemed as impervious as ever to the pathos of his position in having thrown himself and his good looks away upon a plain woman six or seven years older than himself. All these things passed quickly through his mind, as if they found an accustomed groove there, and mingled acidly with the disturbing sub-consciousness that the mare would inevitably come home with a sore back if her rider did not sit straighter than she was doing at present.

" Look here, Francie," he said at last, with something of asperity, " it's all very fine to humbug now, but if you don't take care you'll find yourself in the county court some fine day. It's easier to get there than you'd think," he added gloomily, " and then there'll be the devil to pay, and nothing to pay him with ; and what'll you do then ? "

"I'll send for you to come and bail me out ! " replied Francie without hesitation, giving an unconsidered whack behind the saddle as she spoke. The black mare at once showed her sense of the liberty by kicking up her heels in a manner that lifted Francie a hand's-breadth from her seat, and shook her foot out of the stirrup. " Gracious ! " she gasped, when she had sufficiently recovered herself to speak ;

.

" what did he do ? Did he buck-jump? Oh, Mr. Lambert—" as the mare, satisfied with her protest, broke into a sharp trot, " do stop him, I can't get my foot into the stirrup ! "

Lambert, trotting serenely beside her on his tall chestnut, watched her precarious bumpings for a minute or two with a grin, then he stretched out a capable hand, and pulled the mare into a walk.

" Now, where would you be without me ? " he inquired.

" Sitting on the road," replied Francie. " I never felt such a horrid rough thing—and look at Mrs. Lambert looking at me over the wall ! Weren't you a cad that you wouldn't stop him before."

In the matter of exercise, Mrs. Lambert was one of those people who want but little here below, nor want that little long. The tour of the two acres that formed the demesne of Rosemount was generally her limit, and any spare energy that remained to her after that perambulation was spent in taking weeds out of the garden path with a lady-like cane-handled spud. This implement was now in her gauntletted hand, and she waved it feebly to the riders as they

passed, while Muffy stood in front of her and barked
with asthmatic fury.

"Make Miss Fitzpatrick come in to tea on her
way home, Roderick." she called, looking admiringly
at the girl with kind eyes that held no spark of
jealousy of her beauty and youth. Mrs. Lambert was
one of the women who sink prematurely and unresist-
ingly into the sloughs of middle-age. For her there
had been no intermediary period of anxious tracking
of grey hairs, of fevered energy in the playing of
lawn-tennis and rounders ; she had seen, with a feeling too sluggish to be respected as resignation, her
complexion ascend the scale of colour from passable
pink to the full sunset flush that now burned in her
cheeks and spanned the sharp ridge of her nose ; and
she still, as she had always done, bought her expen-
sive Sunday bonnet as she would have bought a piece
of furniture, because it was handsome, not because it
was becoming. The garden hat which she now wore
could not pretend to either of these qualifications,
and, as Francie looked at her, the contrast between
her and her husband was as conspicuous as even he
could have wished.

Francie's first remark, however, after they had passed by, seemed to show that her point of view was not the same as his.

" Won't she be very lonely there all the afternoon by herself ? " she asked, with a backward glance at the figure in the garden hat.

" Oh, not she ! " said Lambert carelessly, " she has the dog, and she'll potter about there as happy as possible. She's all right." Then after a pause, in which the drift of Francie's question probably presented itself to him for the first time, " I wish everyone was as satisfied with their life as she is "

" How bad you are ! " returned Francie, quite unmoved by the gloomily sentimental roll of Mr. Lambert's eyes. " I never heard a man talk such nonsense in my life ! "

" My dear child," said Lambert, with paternal melancholy, " when you're my age— "

" Which I sha'n't be for the next fifteen years—" interrupted Francie.

Mr. Lambert checked himself abruptly, and looked cross.

" Oh, all right ! If you're going to sit on me

every time I open my mouth, I'd better shut up."

Francie with some difficulty brought the black mare beside the chestnut, and put her hand for an instant on Lambert's arm.

" Ah now, don't be angry with me ! " she said, with a glance whose efficacy she had often proved in similar cases, " you know I was only funning."

" I am not in the least angry with you," replied Lambert coldly, though his eyes turned in spite of himself to her face.

" Oh, I know very well you're angry with me," rejoined Francie, with unfeigned enjoyment of the situation ; " your mustash always gets as black as a coal when you're angry."

The adornment referred to twitched, but its owner said nothing.

" There now, you're laughing ! " continued Francie, " but it's quite true ; I remember the first time I noticed, that was the time you brought Mrs. Lambert up to town about her teeth, and you took places at the Gaiety for the three of us—and oh ! do you remember—" leaning back and laughing wholeheartedly, " she couldn't get her teeth in in time, and you wanted her to go without any, and she wouldn't, for fear she might laugh at the pantomime, and I had promised to go to the Dalkey Band that night with the Whittys, and then when you got up to our house and found you'd got the three tickets for nothing, you were so mad that when I came down into the parlour I declare I thought you'd been dye-ing your mustash! Aunt Tish said afterwards it was because your face got so white, but *I* knew it was because you were in such a passion."

" Well, I didn't like chucking away fifteen shillings a bit more than anyone else would," said Lambert.

" Ah, well, we made it up, d'ye remember," said Francie, regarding him with a laughing eye, in which there was a suspicion of sentiment; "and after all you were able to change the tickets to another night, and it was ' Pinafore,' and you laughed at me so awfully, because I cried at the part where the two lovers are saying good-bye to each other, and poor Mrs. Lambert got her teeth in in a hurry to go with us, and she couldn't utter the whole night for fear they'd fall out."

Perhaps the allusions to his wife's false teeth had a subtly soothing effect on Mr. Lambert. He never was averse to anything that showed that other people were as conscious as he was of the disparity between his own admirable personal equipment and that of Mrs. Lambert ; it was another admission of the great fact that he had thrown himself away. His eyebrows and moustache became less truculent, he let himself down with a complacent sarcasm on Francie's method of holding her whip, and, as they rode on, he permitted to himself the semi-proprietary enjoyment of an agent in pointing out boundaries, and landmarks, and improvements.

They had ridden at first under a pale green arch of road-side trees, with fields on either side full of buttercups and dog-daisies, a land of pasture and sleek cattle, and neat stone walls. But in the second or third mile the face of the country changed. The blue lake that had lain in the distance like a long slab of lapis lazuli, was within two fields of them now, moving drowsily in and out of the rocks, and over the coarse gravel of its shore. The trees had dwindled to ragged hazel and thorn bushes ; the fat

cows of the comfortable farms round Lismoyle
were replaced by lean, dishevelled goats, and shelves
and flags of gray limestone began to contest the
right of the soil with the thin grass and the wiry
brushwood. We have said gray limestone, but that
hard-worked adjective cannot at all express the cold,
pure blueness that these boulders take, under the
sky of summer. Some word must yet be coined in
which neither blue nor lilac shall have the suprem-
acy, and in which the steely purple of a pigeon's
breast shall not be forgotten.

The rock was everywhere. Even the hazels were
at last squeezed out of existence, and inland, over the
slowly swelling hills, it lay like the pavement of
some giant city, that had been jarred from its sym-
metry by an earthquake. A mile away on the
further side of this iron belt, a clump of trees rose
conspicuously by the lake side, round a two-storied
white house, and towards these trees the road wound
its sinuous way. The grass began to show in larger
and larger patches between the rocks, and the in-
domitable hazels crept again out of the crannies, and
raised their low canopies over the heads of the

browsing sheep and goats. A stream, brown with turf-mould, and fierce with battles with the boulders, made a boundary between the stony wilderness and the dark green pastures of Gurthnamuckla. It dashed under a high-backed little bridge with such excitement that the black mare, for all her intelligence, curved her neck, and sidled away from the parapet towards Lambert's horse.

Just beyond the bridge, a repulsive looking old man was sitting on a heap of stones, turning over the contents of a dirty linen pouch. Beside him were an empty milk-can, and a black and white dog which had begun by trying to be a collie, and had relapsed into an indifferent attempt at a greyhound. It greeted the riders with the usual volley of barking, and its owner let fall some of the coppers that he was counting over, in his haste to strike at it with the long stick that was lying beside him.

"Have done! Sailor! Blasht yer sowl! Have done!" then, with honeyed obsequiousness, "yer honour's welcome, Mr. Lambert."

"Is Miss Duffy in the house?" asked Lambert.

"She is, she is, yer honour," he answered, in the

nasal mumble peculiar to his class, getting up and beginning to shuffle after the horses, "but what young lady is this at all? Isn't she very grand, God bless her!"

"She's Miss Fitzpatrick, Miss Mullen's cousin, Billy," answered Lambert graciously; approbation could not come from a source too low for him to be susceptible to it.

The old man came up beside Francie, and, clutching the skirt of her habit, blinked at her with sly and swimming eyes.

"Fitzpathrick is it? Begob I knew her grannema well; she was a fine hearty woman, the Lord have mercy on her! And she never seen me without she'd give me a shixpence or maybe a shillin'."

Francie was skilled in the repulse of the Dublin beggar, but this ancestral precedent was something for which she was not prepared. The clutch tightened on her habit and the disgusting old face almost touched it, as Billy pressed close to her, mouthing out incomprehensible blessings and entreaties. She felt afraid of his red eyes and clawing fingers, and she turned helplessly to Lambert.

"Here, be off now, Billy, you old fool!" he said; "we've had enough of you. Run and open the gate."

The farm-house, with its clump of trees, was close to them, and its drooping iron entrance gate shrieked resentfully as the old man dragged it open.

CHAPTER VII.

MISS JULIA DUFFY, the tenant of Gurthnamuckla, was a woman of few friends. The cart track that led to her house was covered with grass, except for two brown ruts and a narrow footpath in the centre, and the boughs of the sycamores that grew on either side of it drooped low as if ignoring the possibility of a visitor. The house door remained shut from year's end to year's end, contrary to the usual kindly Irish custom ; in fact, its rotten timbers were at once supported and barricaded by a diagonal beam that held them together, and was itself beginning to rot under its shroud of cobwebs. The footpath skirted the duckpond in front of the door, and led round the corner of the house to what had been in the palmy days of Gurthnamuckla the stableyard, and wound through its weedy heaps of dirt to the kitchen door.

84

Julia Duffy, looking back through the squalors of some sixty years, could remember the days when the hall door used to stand open from morning till night, and her father's guests were many and thirsty, almost as thirsty as he, though perhaps less persistently so. He had been a hard-drinking Protestant farmer, who had married his own dairywoman, a Roman Catholic, dirty, thriftless, and a cousin of Norry the Boat ; and he had so disintegrated himself with whisky that his body and soul fell asunder at what was considered by his friends to be the premature age of seventy-two. Julia had always been wont to go to Lismoyle church with her father, not so much as a matter of religious as of social conviction. All the best bonnets in the town went to the parish church, and to a woman of Julia's stamp, whose poor relations wear hoods and shawls over their heads and go to chapel, there is no salvation out of a bonnet. After old John Duffy's death, however, bonnets and the aristocratic way of salvation seemed together to rise out of his daughter's scope. Chapel she despised with all the fervour of an Irish Protestant, but if the farm was to be kept and the rent paid, there was no

money to spare for bonnets. Therefore Julia, in
defiance of the entreaties of her mother's priest and
her own parson, would have nothing of either chapel
or church, and stayed sombrely at home. Marriage
had never come near her; in her father's time the
necessary dowry had not been forthcoming, and even
her ownership of the farm was not enough to
counterbalance her ill-looks and her pagan habits.

As in a higher grade of society science sometimes
steps in when religion fails, so, in her moral isolation,
Julia Duffy turned her attention to the mysteries of
medicine and the culture of herbs. By the time her
mother died she had established a position as doctor
and wise woman, which was immensely abetted by
her independence of the ministrations of any church.
She was believed in by the people, but there was no
liking in the belief; when they spoke to her they
called her Miss Duffy, in deference to a now im-
palpable difference in rank as well as in recognition
of her occult powers, and they kept as clear of her
as they conveniently could. The payment of her
professional services was a matter entirely in the
hands of the people themselves, and ranged, accord-

ing to the circumstances of the case, from a score of
eggs or a can of buttermilk, to a crib of turf or " the
makings " of a homespun flannel petticoat. Where
there was the possibility of a fee it never failed ;
where there was not, Julia Duffy gave her " yerreb
tay " (*i.e.*, herb tea) and Holloway's pills without
question or hesitation.

No one except herself knew how vital these offerings were to her. The farm was still hers, and, perhaps, in all her jealous, unsunned nature, the only
note of passion was her feeling for the twenty acres
that, with the house, remained to her of her father's
possessions. She had owned the farm for twenty
years now, and had been the abhorrence and the despair of each successive Bruff agent. The land went
from bad to worse ; ignorance, neglect, and poverty
are a formidable conjunction even without the moral
support that the Land League for a few years had
afforded her, and Miss Duffy tranquilly defied Mr.
Lambert, offering him at intervals such rent as she
thought fitting, while she sub-let her mossy, deterior-
ated fields to a Lismoyle grazier. Perhaps her
nearest approach to pleasure was the time at the

beginning of each year when she received and dealt
with the offers for the grazing ; then she tasted
the sweets of ownership, and then she conde-
scended to dole out to Mr. Lambert such payment
"on account" as she deemed advisable, confronting
his remonstrances with her indisputable poverty, and
baffling his threats with the recital of a promise that
she should never be disturbed in her father's farm,
made to her, she alleged, by Sir Benjamin Dysart,
when she entered upon her inheritance.

There had been a time when a barefooted serving-
girl had suffered under Miss Duffy's rule ; but for the
last few years the times had been bad, the price of
grazing had fallen, and the mistress's temper and the
diet having fallen in a corresponding ratio, the bond-
woman had returned to her own people and her
father's house, and no successor had been found to
take her place. That is to say, no recognised successor. But, as fate would have it, on the very day
that "Moireen Rhu" had wrapped her shawl about
her head, and stumped, with cursings, out of the
house of bondage, the vague stirrings that regulate
the perambulations of beggars had caused Billy

Grainy to resolve upon Gurthnamuckla as the place where he would, after the manner of his kind, ask for a wallet full of potatoes and a night's shelter. A week afterwards he was still there, drawing water, bringing in turf, feeding the cow, and receiving, in return for these offices, his board and lodging and the daily dressing of a sore shin which had often coerced the most uncharitable to hasty and nauseated almsgiving. The arrangement glided into permanency, and Billy fell into a life of lazy routine that was preserved from stagnation by a daily expedition to Lismoyle to sell milk for Miss Duffy, and to do a little begging on his own account.

Gurthnamuckla had still about it some air of the older days when Julia Duffy's grandfather was all but a gentleman, and her drunken father and dairymaid mother were in their cradles. The tall sycamores that bordered the cart track were witnesses to the time when it had been an avenue, and the lawn-like field was yellow in spring with the daffodils of a former civilisation. The tops of the trees were thick with nests, and the grave cawing of rooks made a background of mellow, serious respect-

ability that had its effect even upon Francie. She
said something to this intent as she and Lambert
jogged along the grass by the track.

" Nice ! " returned her companion with enthusiasm,
I should think it was ! I'd make that one of the
sweetest little places in the country if I had it.
There's no better grass for young horses anywhere,
and there's first-class stabling. I can tell you you're
not the only one that thinks it's a nice place," he
continued, " but this old devil that has it won't give
it up ; she'd rather let the house rot to pieces over
her head than go out of it."

They rode past the barricaded hall door, and
round the corner of the house into the yard, and
Lambert called for Miss Duffy for some time in
vain. Nothing responded except the turkey cock,
who answered each call with an infuriated gobble,
and a donkey, who, in the dark recesses of a cow-
house, lifted up his voice in heartrending rejoinder.
At last a window fell down with a bang in the upper
story, and the mistress of the house put out her
head. Francie had only time to catch a glimpse of
a thin, dirty face, a hooked nose, and unkempt black

hair, before the vision was withdrawn, and a slipshod step was heard coming downstairs.

When Miss Duffy appeared at her kitchen door she had flung a shawl round her head, possibly to conceal the fact that her crinkled mat of hair held thick in it, like powder, the turf ashes of many sluttish days. Her stained and torn black skirt had evidently just been unpinned from about her waist, and was hitched up at one side, showing a frayed red Galway petticoat, and that her feet had recently been thrust into her boots was attested by the fact that their laces trailed on the ground beside her. In spite of these disadvantages, however, it was with a manner of the utmost patronage that she greeted Mr. Lambert.

"I would ask you and the young leedy to dismount," she continued in the carefully genteel voice that she clung to in the wreck of her fortunes, " but I am, as' you will see," she made a gesture with a dingy hand, "quite 'in dishabilly' as they say; I've been a little indisposed, and—"

" Oh, no matter, Miss Duffy," interrupted Lambert, " I only wanted to say a few words to you on business, and Miss Fitzpatrick will ride about the place till we're done."

Miss Duffy's small black eyes turned quickly to Francie.

" Oh, indeed, is that Miss Fitzpatrick ? My fawther knew her grandfawther. I am much pleased to make her acquaintance."

She inclined her head as she spoke, and Francie, with much disposition to laugh, bowed hers in return ; each instant Miss Duffy's resemblance, both in feature and costume, to a beggar woman who frequented the corner of Sackville Street, was becoming harder to bear with fortitude, and she was delighted to leave Lambert to his *tête-à-tête* and ride out into the lawn, among the sycamores and hawthorns, where the black mare immediately fell to devouring grass with a resolve that was quite beyond Francie's power to combat.

She broke a little branch off a low-growing ash tree, to keep away the flies that were doing their best to spoil the pleasure of a perfect afternoon, and sat there, fanning herself lazily, while the mare, with occasional impatient tugs at the reins and stampings at the flies, cropped her way onwards from one luscious tuft to another. The Lismoyle grazier's cattle had collected themselves under the trees at the farther end of the lawn where a swampy pool still remained of the winter encroachments of the lake. In the sunshine at the other side of the wall a chain of such pools stretched to the broad blue water, and grey limestone rocks showed above the tangle of hemlock and tall spikes of magenta foxgloves. A white sail stood dazzlingly out in the turquoise blue of a band of calm, and the mountains on the farther side of the lake were palely clothed in thinnest lavender and most ethereal green.

It might have been the unexpected likeness that she had found in Julia Duffy to her old friend the beggar woman that took Francie's thoughts away . from this idyll of perfected summer to the dry, grey Dublin streets that had been her uttermost horizon a week ago. The milkman generally called at the Fitzpatricks' house at about this hour ; the clank of his pint measure against the area railings, even his pleasantries with Maggie the cook, relative to his bestowing an extra " sup for the cat," were suddenly and sharply present with her. The younger Fitz-patrick children would be home from school, and would be raging through the kitchen seeking what they might devour in the interval before the six o'clock dinner, and she herself would probably have been engaged in a baking game of tennis in the square outside her uncle's house. She felt very sorry for Aunt Tish when she thought of that hungry gang of sons and daughters and of the evil days that had come upon the excellent and respectable Uncle Robert, and the still more evil days that would come in another fortnight or so, when the whole bursting party had squeezed themselves into a little house at Bray, there to exist for an indefinite period on Irish stew, strong tea, and a diminished income. There was a kind of understanding that when they were "settled" she was to go back to them, and blend once more her five and twenty pounds a year with the Fitzpatrick funds; but this afternoon, with the rich summer stillness and the blaze of buttercups all about her, and the unfamiliar feeling of the mare's restless shoulder under her knee, she was exceed-ingly glad that the settling process would take some months at least. She was not given to introspection, and could not have said anything in the least interesting about her mental or moral atmosphere : she was too uneducated and too practical for any self-communings of this kind ; but she was quite certain of two things, that in spite of her affection for the Fitzpatricks she was very glad she was not going to spend the summer in Dublin or Bray, and also, that in spite of certain bewildering aspects of her cousin Charlotte, she was beginning to have what she defined to herself as " a high old time."

It was somewhere about this period in her meditations that she became aware of a slight swishing and puffing sound from the direction of the lake, and a steam-launch came swiftly along close under the shore. She was a smart-looking boat, spick and span as white paint and a white funnel with a brass band could make her, and in her were seated two men, one, radiant in a red and white blazer, was steering, while the other, in clothes to which even distance failed to lend enchantment, was menially engaged in breaking coals with a hammer. The boughs of the trees intervened exasperatingly be-

tween Francie and this glittering vision, and the
resolve to see it fully lent her the power to drag the
black mare from her repast, and urge her forward to
an opening where she could see and be seen, two
equally important objects.

She had instantly realised that these were those
heroes of romance, " the Lismoyle officers," the pro-
babilities of her alliance with one of whom had been
the subject of some elegant farewell badinage on the
part of her bosom friend, Miss Fanny Hemphill.
Francie's acquaintance with the British army had
hitherto been limited to one occasion when, at a
Sandymount evening band, " one of the officers from
Beggars' Bush Barracks "—so she had confided‚ to
Miss Hemphill—had taken off his hat to her, and
been very polite until Aunt Tish had severely told
him that no true gentleman would converse with a
lady without she was presented to him, and had in-
continently swept her home. She could see them
quite plainly now, and from the fact that the man
who had been rooting among the coals was now sitting up, evidently at the behest of the steersman, and
looking at her, it was clear that she had attracted at-

tention too. Even the black mare pricked her ears, and stared at this new kind of dragon-fly creature that went noisily by, leaving a feathery smear on the air behind it, and just then Mr. Lambert rode out of the stableyard, and looked about him for his charge.

" Francie !" he called with perceptible impatience ; " what are you at down there ? "

The steam-launch had by this time passed the opening, and Francie turned and rode towards him. Her hat was a good deal on the back of her head, and her brilliant hair caught the sunshine ; the charm of her supple figure atoned for the crookedness of her seat, and her eyes shone with an excitement born of the delightful sight of soldiery.

" Oh, Mr. Lambert, weren't those the officers ? " she cried, as he rode up to her ; " which was which ? Haven't they a grand little steamer ? "

Lambert's temper had apparently not been improved by his conversation with Julia Duffy ; instead of answering Miss Fitzpatrick he looked at her with a clouded brow, and in his heart he said, " Damn the officers ! "

" I wondered which of them was the captain," continued Francie; "I suppose it was the little fair one; he was much the best dressed, and he was making the other one do all the work."

Lambert gave a scornful laugh.

"I'll leave you to find that out for yourself. I'll engage it won't be long before you know all about them. You've made a good start already."

"Oh, very well," replied Francie, letting fall both her reins in order to settle her hat; "some day you'll be asking me something, and I won't tell you, and then you'll be sorry."

"Some day you'll be breaking your neck, and then *you'll* be sorry," retorted Lambert, taking up the fallen reins.

They rode out to the gate of Gurthnamuckla in silence, and after a mile of trotting, which was to Francie a period of mingled pain and anxiety, the horses slackened of their own accord, and began to pick their way gingerly over the smooth sheets of rock that marked the entry of the road into the stony tract mentioned in the last chapter. Francie took the opportunity for a propitiatory question.

"What were you and the old woman talking

about all that time? I thought you were never coming."

"Business," said Lambert shortly; then viciously, "if any conversation with a woman can ever be called business."

"Oho! then you couldn't get her to do what you wanted!" laughed Francie; "very good for you too! I think you always get your own way."

"Is that your opinion?" said Lambert, turning his dark eyes upon her; "I'm sorry I can't agree with you."

The fierce heat had gone out of the afternoon as they passed along the lonely road, through the country of rocks and hazel bushes; the sun was sending low flashes into their eyes from the bright mirror of the lake; the goats that hopped uncomfortably about in the enforced and detested *tête-à-tête* caused by a wooden yoke across their necks, cast blue shadows of many-legged absurdity on the warm slabs of stone; a carrion crow, swaying on the thin topmost bough of a thorn-bush, a blot in the mellow afternoon sky, was looking about him if haply he could see a wandering kid whose eyes would serve him for his supper; and a couple of miles away, at Rosemount, Mrs. Lambert was sending down to be kept hot what she and Charlotte had left of the Sally Lunn.

Francie was not sorry when she found herself again under the trees of the Lismoyle highroad, and in spite of the injuries which the pommels of the saddle were inflicting upon her, and the growing stiffness of all her muscles, she held gallantly on at a sharp trot, till her hair-pins and her hat were loosed from their foundations, and her green habit rose in ungainly folds. They were nearing Rosemount when they heard wheels behind them; Lambert took the left side of the road, and the black mare followed his example with such suddenness, that Francie, when she had recovered her equilibrium, could only be thankful that nothing more than her hat had come off. With the first instinct of woman she snatched at the coils of hair that fell down her back and hung enragingly over her eyes, and tried to wind them on to her head again; she became horribly aware that a waggonette with several people in it had pulled up beside her, and, finally, that a young man with a clean - shaved face and an eyeglass was handing her her hat and taking off his own.

Holding in her teeth the few hair-pins that she had been able to save from the wreck, she stammered a gratitude that she was far from feeling; and when she heard Lambert say, " Oh, thank you, Dysart, you just saved me getting off," she felt that her discomfiture was complete.

CHAPTER VIII.

CHRISTOPHER DYSART was a person about whom Lismoyle and its neighbourhood had not been able to come to a satisfactory conclusion, unless indeed, that conclusion can be called satisfactory which admitted him to be a disappointment. From the time that, as a shy, plain, little boy he first went to a school, and, after the habit of boys, ceased to exist except in theory and holidays, a steady undercurrent of interest had always set about him. His mother was so charming, and his father so delicate, and he himself so conveniently contemporary with so many daughters, that although the occasional glimpses vouchsafed of him during his Winchester and Oxford career were as discouraging as they were brief, it was confidently expected that he would emerge from his boyish shyness when he came to take his proper place in the county and settle down at Bruff. Thus Lady Eyrefield, and Mrs. Waller, and their like, the careful mothers of those contemporaneous daughters, and thus also, after their kind, the lesser ladies of Lismoyle.

But though Christopher was now seven and twenty he seemed as far from "taking his place in the county" as he had ever been. His mother's friends had no particular fault to find with him ; that was a prominent feature in their dissatisfaction. He was quite good-looking enough for an eldest son, and his politeness to their daughters left them nothing to complain of except the discouraging fact that it was exceeded by his politeness to themselves. His readiness to talk when occasion demanded was undisputed, but his real or pretended dulness in those matters of local interest, which no one except an outsider calls gossip, made conversation with him a hollow and heartless affair. One of his most exasperating points was that he could not be referred to any known type. He was "between the sizes," as shopmen say of gloves. He was not smart and aggressive enough for the soldiering type, nor sporting e

gentleman, but neither had

attentiveness of the ideal curat

be lightly disposed of as an ecc

have been some sort of consolat

"If I ever could have i

Dysart's son would have turne

the Dowager Lady Eyrefiel

bitterness, "I should not ha

trouble of writing to Castlemo

out as his secretary. I thoug

and dinner parties would h:

for him, but though they polis

and improved that most pai

stutter, he's at heart just as mu

Lismoyle was, according t

nonplussed. Mrs. Baker had i

it was sending him to these

versities, instead of to Trin

that had taken the fun out

know what with the heat. Mrs. Corkran, the widow
of the late rector of Lismoyle, had, however, rejoined
that she had always found Mr. Dysart a most
humble-minded young man on the occasions 'when
she had met him at his cousin Mrs. Gascogne's,
and by no means puffed up with his rank or
learning. This proposition Mrs. Baker had not
attempted to dispute, but none the less she had
felt it to be beside the point. She had not found
that Christopher's learning had disposed him to
come to her tennis parties, and she did not feel
humility to be a virtue that graced a young man
of property. Certainly, in spite of his humility,
she could not venture to take him to task for his
neglect of her entertainments as she could Mr.
Hawkins; but then it is still more certain that
Christopher would not, as Mr. Hawkins had often
done, sit down before her, as before a walled
town, and so skilfully entreat her that in five minutes
all would have been forgiven and forgotten.

It was perhaps an additional point of aggravation
that, dull and unprofitable though he was considered
to be, Christopher had amusements of his own in

which the neighbourhood had no part. Since he had
returned from the West Indies, his three-ton cutter
with the big Una sail had become one of the features
of the lake, but though a red parasol was often pictur-
esquely visible above the gunwale, the knowledge
that it sheltered his sister deprived it of the almost
painful interest that it might otherwise have had, and
at the same time gave point to a snub that was un-
intentionally effective and comprehensive. There
were many sunny mornings on which Mr. Dysart's
camera occupied commanding positions in the town,
or its outskirts, while its owner photographed groups
of old women and donkeys, regardless of the fact
that Miss Kathleen Baker, in her most becoming hat,
had taken her younger sister from the schoolroom to
play a showy game of lawn-tennis in the garden in
front of her father's villa, or was, with Arcadian
industry, cutting buds off the roses that dropped their
pink petals over the low wall on to the road. It was
quite inexplicable that the photographer should pack
up his camera and walk home without taking
advantage of this artistic opportunity beyond a civil
lift of his cap ; and at such times Miss Baker would

re-enter the villa with a feeling of contempt for Mr. Dysart that was almost too deep for words.

She might have been partially consoled had she known that on a June morning not long after the latest of these repulses, her feelings were fully shared by the person whom, for the last two Sundays, she had looked at in the Dysart pew with a respectful dislike that implied the highest compliment in her power. Miss Evelyn Hope-Drummond stood at the bow-window of the Bruff drawing-room and looked out over the gravelled terrace, across the flower-garden and the sunk fence, to the clump of horse chestnuts by the lake-side. Beyond these the cattle were standing knee-deep in the water, and on the flat margin a pair of legs in white flannel trousers was all that the guest, whom his mother delighted to honour, could see of Christopher Dysart. The remainder of him wrestled beneath a black velvet pall with the helplessly wilful legs of his camera, and all his mind, as Miss Hope-Drummond well knew, was concentrated upon cows. Her first visit to Ireland was proving less amusing than she had expected, she thought, and as she watched Christopher she wished fervently that she had not offered to carry any of his horrid things across the park for him. In the flower-garden below the terrace she could see Lady Dysart and Pamela in deep consultation over an infirm rose-tree; a wheelbarrow full of pans of seedlings sufficiently indicated what their occupation would be for the rest of the morning, and she felt it was of a piece with the absurdities of Irish life that the ladies of the house should enjoy doing the gardener's work for him. The strong scent of heated Gloire de Dijon roses came through the window, and suggested to her how well one of them would suit with her fawn-coloured Redfern gown, and she leaned out to pick a beautiful bud that was swaying in the sun just within reach.

"Ha—a—ah! I see ye, missy! Stop picking my flowers! Push, James Canavan, you devil, you! Push!"

A bath-chair, occupied by an old man in a tall hat, and pushed by a man also in a tall hat, had suddenly turned the corner of the house, and Miss . Hope-Drummond drew back precipitately to avoid the up-lifted walking-stick of Sir Benjamin Dysart.

"Oh, fie, for shame, Sir Benjamin!" exclaimed the man who had been addressed as James Canavan. "Pray, cull the rose, miss," he continued, with a flourish of his hand; "sweets to the sweet!"

Sir Benjamin aimed a backward stroke with his oak stick at his attendant, a stroke in which long practice had failed to make him perfect, and in the exchange of further amenities the party passed out of sight. This was not Miss Hope-Drummond's first meeting with her host. His bath-chair had daily, as it seemed to her, lain in wait in the shrubberies, to cause terror to the solitary, and discomfiture to *tête-à-têtes;* and on one morning he had stealthily protruded the crook of his stick from the door of his room as she went by, and all but hooked her round the ankle with it.

"Really, it is disgraceful that he is not locked up," she said to herself crossly, as she gathered the contested bud, and sat down to write letters; "but in Ireland no one seems to think anything of anything!"

It was very hot down in the garden where Lady Dysart and Pamela were at work; Lady Dysart kneeling in the inadequate shade of a parasol, whose handle she had propped among the pans in the wheelbarrow, and Pamela weeding a flower-bed a few yards away. It was altogether a scene worthy in its domestic simplicity of the Fairchild Family only that instead of Mr. Fairchild, " stretched on the grass at a little distance with his book," a bronze-coloured dachshund lay roasting his long side in the sun ; and also that Lady Dysart, having mistaken the young chickweed in a seedling pan for the asters that should have been there, was filling her bed symmetrically with the former, an imbecility that Mrs. Sherwood would never have permitted in a parent. The mother and daughter lifted their heads at the sound of the conflict on the terrace.

" Papa will frighten Evelyn into a fit," observed Pamela, rubbing a midge off her nose with an earthy gardening glove; " I wish James Canavan could be induced to keep him away from the house."

" It's all right, dear," said Lady Dysart, panting a little as she straightened her back and surveyed her rows of chickweed ; " Christopher is with her, and you know he never notices anyone else when Christopher is there."

Lady Dysart had in her youth married, with a little judicious coercion, a man thirty years older than herself, and after a long and, on the whole, extremely unpleasant period of matrimony, she was now enjoying a species of Indian summer, dating from six years back, when Christopher's coming of age and the tenants' rejoicings thereat, had caused such a paroxysm of apoplectic jealousy on the part of Christopher's father as, combining with the heat of the day, had brought on "a stroke." Since then the bath-chair and James Canavan had mercifully intervened between him and the rest of the world, and his offspring were now able to fly before him with a frankness and success impossible in the old days.

Pamela did not answer her mother at once.

"Do you know I'm afraid Christopher isn't with her," she said, looking both guilty and perturbed.

Lady Dysart groaned aloud.

"Why, where is he?" she demanded "I left Evelyn helping him to paste in photographs after breakfast; I thought that would have been nice occupation for them for at least two hours ; but as for Christopher—" she continued, her voice deepening to declamation, " it is quite hopeless to expect anything from him. I should rather trust Garry to entertain anyone. The day *he* took her out in the boat they weren't in till six o'clock ! "

" That was because Garry ran the punt on the shallow, and they had to wade ashore and walk all the way round."

" That has nothing to say to it ; at all events they had something to talk about when they came back, which is more than Christopher has when he has been out sailing. It is *most* disheartening ; I ask nice girls to the house, but I might just as well ask nice boys—Oh, of course, yes—" in answer to a protest from her daughter; " he *talks* to them ; but you know quite well what I mean."

This complaint was not the first indication of Lady Dysart's sentiments about this curious son whom she had produced. She was a clever woman, a renowned solver of the acrostics in her society paper, and a holder of strong opinions as to the prophetic meaning of the Pyramids ; but Christopher

was an acrostic in a strange language, an enigma beyond her sphere. She had a vague but rooted feeling that young men were normally in love with
somebody, or at least pretending to be so ; it was, of
course, an excellent thing that Christopher did not
lose his heart to the wrong people, but she would
probably have preferred the agitation of watching his
progress through the most alarming flirtations to the
security that deprived conversation with other
mothers of much of its legitimate charm.

" Well, there was Miss Fetherstone," began Pamela
after a moment of obvious consideration.

" Miss Fetherstone ! " echoed Lady Dysart in her
richest contralto, fixing eyes of solemn reproach upon
her daughter ; " do you suppose that for one instant I
thought there was anything in that ? No baby, no
idiot baby, could have believed in it ! "

" Well, I don't know," said Pamela ; " I think you
and Mrs. Waller believed in it, at least I remember
your both settling what your wedding presents were
to be ! "

" *I* never said a word about wedding presents, it
was Mrs. Waller ! Of course she was anxious about

her own niece, just as *anybody* would have been
under the circumstances." Lady Dysart here became aware of something in Pamela's expression
that made her add hurriedly, " Not that *I* ever had
the faintest shadow of belief in it. Too well do I
know Christopher's platonic philanderings ; and you
see the affair turned out just as I said it would.

Pamela refrained from pursuing her advantage.

" If you like I'll make him come with Evelyn and
me to the choir practice this afternoon," she said
after a pause. " Of course he'll hate it, poor boy,
especially as Miss Mullen wrote to me the other day
and asked us to come to tea after it was over."

" Oh, yes ! " said Lady Dysart with sudden interest and forgetfulness of her recent contention,
"and you will see the new importation whom we
met with Mr. Lambert the other day. What a
charming young creature she looked ! ' The fair one
with the golden locks ' was the only description for
her ! And yet that miserable Christopher will only
say that she is ' chocolate-boxey ! ' Oh ! I have no
patience with Christopher's affectation ! " she ended,
rising from her knees and brushing the earth from

her extensive lap with a gesture of annoyance. She began to realise that the sun was hot and luncheon late, and it was at this unpropitious moment that Pamela, having finished the flower-bed she had been weeding, approached the scene of her mother's labours.

"Mamma," she said faintly, "you have planted the whole bed with chickweed!"

CHAPTER IX.

IT had been hard work pulling the punt across from
Bruff to Lismoyle with two well-grown young women
sitting in the stern; it had been a hot walk up from
the landing-place to the church, but worse than these,
transcendentally worse, in that it involved the suffering of the mind as well as the body, was the choir
practice. Christopher's long nose drooped despond-
ingly over his Irish church hymnal, and his long
back had a disconsolate hoop in it as he leaned it
against the wall in his place in the backmost row of
the choir benches. The chants had been long and
wearisome, and the hymns were proving themselves
equally enduring. Christopher was not eminently
musical or conspicuously religious, and he regarded
with a kind of dismal respect and surprise the fervour
in Pamela's pure profile as she turned to Mrs.
Gascogne and suggested that the hymn they had

116

just gone through twice should be sung over again.
He supposed it was because she had High Church
tendencies that she was able to stand this sort of
thing, and his mind drifted into abstract speculations
as to how people could be as good as Pamela was
and live.

In the interval before the last hymn he derived a
temporary solace from finding his own name inscribed
in dull red characters in the leaf of his hymn-book,
with, underneath in the same colour, the fateful
inscription, " Written in blood by Garrett Dysart."
The thought of his younger brother utilising
pleasantly a cut finger and the long minutes of the
archdeacon's sermon, had for the moment inspired
Christopher with a sympathetic amusement, but he
had relapsed into his pristine gloom. He knew the
hymn perfectly well by this time, and his inoffensive
tenor joined mechanically with the other voices, while
his eyes roamed idly over the two rows of people in
front of him. There was nothing suggestive of
ethereal devotion about Pamela's neighbours. Miss
Mullen's heaving shoulders and extended jaw spoke
of nothing but her determination to out-scream every-

one else ; Miss Hope-Drummond and the curate, on the bench in front of him, were singing primly out of the same hymn-book, the curate obviously frightened, Miss Hope-Drummond as obviously disgusted. The Misses Beattie were furtively eyeing Miss Hope-Drummond's costume ; Miss Kathleen Baker was openly eyeing the curate, whose hymn-book she had been wont to share at happier choir practices, and Miss Fitzpatrick, seated at the end of the row, was watching from the gallery window with unaffected interest the progress of the usual weekly hostilities between Pamela's dachshund and the sexton's cat, and was not even pretending to occupy herself with the business in hand. Christopher's eyes rested on her appraisingly, with the minute observation of short sight, fortified by an eyeglass, and was aware of a small head with a fluffy halo of conventionally golden hair, a straight and slender neck, and an apple-blossom curve of cheek ; he found himself wishing that she would turn a little further round.

The hymn had seven verses, and Pamela and Mrs. Gascogne were going inexorably through them all ; the schoolmaster and schoolmistress, an estimable couple, sole prop of the choir on wet Sundays, were braying brazenly beside him, and this was only the second hymn. Christopher's D sharp melted into a yawn, and before he could screen it with his hymn-book, Miss Fitzpatrick looked round and caught him in the act. A suppressed giggle and a quick lift of the eyebrows instantly conveyed to him that his sentiments were comprehended and sympathised with, and he as instantly was conscious that Miss Mullen was following the direction of her niece's eye. Lady Dysart's children did not share her taste for Miss Mullen ; Christopher vaguely felt some offensive flavour in the sharp smiling glance in which she included him and Francie, and an unexplainable sequence of thought made him suddenly decide that her niece was as second rate as might have been expected.

Never had the choir dragged so hopelessly ; never had Mrs. Gascogne and Pamela compelled their victims to deal with so many and difficult tunes, and never at any previous choir practice had Christopher registered so serious a vow that under no pretext whatever should Pamela entice him there again. They were all sitting down now, while the leaders consulted together about the Kyrie, and the gallery cushions slowly turned to stone in their well-remembered manner. Christopher's ideas of church-going were inseparably bound up with those old gallery cushions. He had sat upon them ever since, as a small boy, he had chirped a treble beside his governess, and he knew every knob in their anatomy. There is something blighting to the devotional tendencies in the atmosphere of a gallery. He had often formulated this theory for his own exculpation, lying flat on his back in a punt in some shady backwater, with the Oxford church bells reminding him reproachfully of Lismoyle Sundays, and of Pamela, the faithful, conscientious Pamela, whipping up the pony to get to church before the bell stopped. Now, after a couple of months' renewed acquaintance with the choir, the theory had hardened into a tedious truism, and when at last Christopher's long legs were free to carry him down the steep stairs, the malign influence of the gallery had brought their owner to the verge of free thought.

He did not know how it had happened or by

whose disposition of the forces it had been brought about, but when Miss Mullen's tea-party detached itself from the other members of the choir at the churchyard gate, Pamela and Miss Hope-Drummond were walking on either side of their hostess, and he was behind with Miss Fitzpatrick.

"You don't appear very fond of hymns, Mr. Dysart," began Francie at once, in the pert Dublin accent that, rightly or wrongly, gives the idea of familiarity.

"People aren't supposed to look about them in church," replied Christopher with the peculiar suavity which, combined with his disconcerting infirmity of pausing before he spoke, had often baffled the young ladies of Barbadoes, and had acquired for him the reputation, perhaps not wholly undeserved, of being a prig.

"Oh, I daresay!" said Francie; "I suppose that's why you sit in the back seat, that no one'll see you doing it!"

There was a directness about this that Lismoyle would not have ventured on, and Christopher looked down at his companion with an increase of interest.

" No ; I sit there because I can go to sleep."

" Well, and do you ? and who do you get to wake you ? "—her quick voice treading sharply on the heels of his quiet one—" I used always to have to sit beside Uncle Robert in church to pinch him at the end of the sermon."

" *I* find it very hard to wake at the end of the sermon too," remarked Christopher, with an experimental curiosity to see what Miss Mullen's unexpected cousin would say next.

" Do y' indeed ? " said Francie, flashing a look at him of instant comprehension and complete *sang froid.* " I'll lend the schoolmistress a hat-pin if you like ! What on earth makes men so sleepy in church I don't know," she continued ; " at our church in Dublin I used to be looking at them. All the gentlemen sit in the corner seat next the aisle, because they're the most comfortable, y' know, and from the minute the clergyman gives out the text—" she made a little gesture with her hand, showing thereby that half the buttons were off her glove— " they're snoring ! "

How young she was, and how pretty, and how

inexpressibly vulgar. Christopher thought all these things in turn, while he did what in him lay to continue the conversation in the manner expected of him. The effort was perhaps not very successful, as, after a few minutes, it was evident that Francie was losing her first freedom of discourse, and was casting about for topics more appropriate to what she had heard of Mr. Dysart's mental and literary standard.

"I hear you're a great photographer, Mr. Dysart," she began. "Miss Mullen says you promised to take a picture of her and her cats, and she was telling me to remind you of it. Isn't it awfully clever of you to be able to do it?"

To this form of question reply is difficult, especially when it is put with all the good faith of complete ignorance. Christopher evaded the imbecilities of direct response.

"I shall think myself awfully clever if I photograph the cats," he said.

"Clever!" she caught him up with a little shriek of laughter. "I can tell you you'll want to be clever! Are you able to photograph up the chimney or under

Norry's bed? for that's where they always run when a man comes into the house, and if you try to stop them they'd claw the face off you! Oh, they're terrors!"

"It's very good of you to tell me all this in time," Christopher said, with a rather absent laugh. He was listening to Miss Mullen's voice, and realising, for the first time, what it would be to live under the same roof with her and her cats; and yet this girl seemed quite light-hearted and happy. "Perhaps, on the whole, I'd better stay away?" he said, looking at her, and feeling in the sudden causeless way in which often the soundest conclusions are arrived at, how vast was the chasm between her ideal of life and his own, and linking with the feeling a pity that would have been self-sufficient if it had not also been perfectly simple.

"Ah! don't say you won't come and take the cats!" Francie exclaimed.

They reached the Tally Ho gate as she spoke, and the others were only a step or two in front of them. Charlotte looked over her shoulder with a benign smile.

"What's this I hear about taking my cats?" she said jovially. "You're welcome to everything in my house, Mr. Dysart, but I'll set the police on you if you take my poor cats!"

"Oh, but I assure you—"

"He's only going to photo them," said Christopher and Francie together.

"Do you hear them, Miss Dysart?" continued Charlotte, fumbling for her latch key, "conspiring together to rob a poor lone woman of her only live stock!"

She opened the door, and as her visitors entered the hall they caught a glance of Susan's large, stern countenance regarding them with concentrated suspicion through the rails of the staircase.

"My beauty-boy!" shouted his mistress, as he vanished upstairs. "Steal him if you can, Mr. Dysart."

Miss Hope-Drummond looked rather more uninterested than is usual in polite society. When she had left the hammock, slung in the shade beside the tennis-ground at Bruff, it had not been to share Mr. Corkran's hymn-book; still less had it been to walk from the church to Tally Ho between Pamela and a woman whom, from having regarded as merely *outrée* and incomprehensible, she had now come to look upon as rather impertinent. Irish society was intolerably mixed, she decided, as she sniffed the various odours of the Tally Ho hall, and, with some sub-connection of ideas, made up her mind that photography was a detestable and silly pursuit for men. While these thoughts were passing beneath her accurately curled fringe, Miss Mullen opened the drawing-room door, and, as they walked in, a short young man in light grey clothes arose from the most comfortable chair to greet them.

There was surprise and disfavour in Miss Mullen's eye as she extended her hand to him.

" This is an unexpected pleasure, Mr. Hawkins," she said.

" Yes," answered Mr. Hawkins cheerfully, taking the hand and doing his best to shake it at the height prescribed by existing fashion, " I thought it would be ; Miss Fitzpatrick asked me to come in this afternoon; didn't you?" addressing himself to Francie. " I got rather a nasty jar when I heard you were all out, but I thought I'd wait for a bit. I knew Miss Dysart always gives 'em fits at the choir practice. All the same, you know, I should have begun to eat the cake if you hadn't come in."

The round table in the middle of the room was spread, in Louisa's accustomed fashion, as if for breakfast, and in the centre was placed a cake, coldly decked in the silver paper trappings that it had long worn in the grocer's window.

"'Twas well for you you didn't!" said Francie, with, as it seemed to Christopher, a most familiar and challenging laugh.

"Why?" inquired Hawkins, looking at her with a responsive eye. "What would you have done?"

"Plenty," returned Francie unhesitatingly; "enough to make you sorry anyway!"

Mr. Hawkins looked delighted, and was opening his mouth for a suitable rejoinder, when Miss Mullen struck in sharply :

"Francie, go tell Louisa that I suppose she expects us to stir our tea with our fingers, for there's not a spoon on the table."

"Oh, let me go," said Hawkins, springing to

open the door; "I know Louisa; she was very kind to me just now. She hunted all the cats out of the room." Francie was already in the hall, and he followed her.

The search for Louisa was lengthy, involving much calling for her by Francie, with falsetto imitations by Mr. Hawkins, and finally a pause, during which it might be presumed that the pantry was being explored. Pamela brought her chair nearer to Miss Mullen, who had begun wrathfully to stir her tea with the sugar-tongs, and entered upon a soothing line of questions as to the health and numbers of the cats; and Christopher, having cut the grocer's cake, and found that it was the usual conglomerate of tallow, saw-dust, bad eggs, and gravel, devoted himself to thick bread and butter, and to conversation with Miss Hope-Drummond. The period of second cups was approaching, when laughter, and a jingle of falling silver in the hall told that the search for Louisa was concluded, and Francie and Mr. Hawkins re-entered the drawing-room, the latter endeavouring, not unsuccessfully, to play the bones with four of Charlotte's best

electro-plated teaspoons, while his brown boots
moved in the furtive rhythm of an imaginary break-
down. Miss Mullen did not even raise her eyes,
and Christopher and Miss Hope-Drummond continued their conversation unmoved; only Pamela
acknowledged the histrionic intention with a sympathetic but nervous smile. Pamela's finger was
always instinctively on the pulse of the person to
whom she was talking, and she knew better than
either Francie or Hawkins that they were in
disgrace.

"I'd be obliged to you for those teaspoons'
Mr. Hawkins, when you've quite done with them,"
said Charlotte, with an ugly look at the chief
offender's self-satisfied countenance; "it's a good
thing no one except myself takes sugar in their
tea."

"We couldn't help it," replied Mr. Hawkins un-
abashed; "Louisa was out for a walk with her young
man, and Miss Fitzpatrick and I had to polish up
the teaspoons ourselves."

Charlotte received this explanation and the teaspoons in silence as she poured out the delinquents,

tea ; there were moments when she permitted herself the satisfaction of showing disapproval if she felt it. Francie accepted her cousin's displeasure philosophically, only betraying her sense of the situation by the expressive eye which she turned towards her companion in disgrace over the rim of her tea-cup. But Mr. Hawkins rose to the occasion. He gulped his tepid and bitter cup of tea with every appearance of enjoyment, and having arranged his small moustache with a silk handkerchief, addressed himself undauntedly to Miss Mullen.

"Do you know I don't believe you have ever been out in our tea-kettle, Miss Mullen. Captain Cursiter and I are feeling very hurt about it."

"If you mean by 'tea-kettle' that steamboat thing that I've seen going about the lake," replied Charlotte, making an effort to resume her first attitude of suave and unruffled hospitality, and at the same time to administer needed correction to Mr. Hawkins, "I certainly have not. I have always been taught that it was manners to wait till you're asked."

"I quite agree with you, Miss Mullen," struck

in Pamela; "we also thought that for a long time, but we had to give it up in the end and ask ourselves! You are much more honoured than we were."

"Oh, I say, Miss Dysart, you know it was only our grovelling humility," expostulated Hawkins, "and you always said it dirtied your frock and spoiled the poetry of the lake. You quite put us off taking anybody out. But we've pulled ourselves together now, Miss Mullen, and if you and Miss Fitzpatrick will fix an afternoon to go down the lake, perhaps if Miss Dysart says she's sorry we'll let her come too, and even, if she's very good, bring whoever she likes with her."

Mr. Hawkins' manner towards ladies had precisely that tone of self-complacent gallantry that Lady Dysart felt to be so signally lacking in her own son, and it was not without its effect even upon Charlotte. It is possible had she been aware that this special compliment to her had been arranged during the polishing of the teaspoons, it might have lost some of its value; but the thought of steaming forth with the Bruff party and "th' officers," under the very noses of the Lismoyle matrons, was the only point of view that presented itself to her.

"Well, I'll give you no answer till I get Mr. Dysart's opinion. He's the only one of you that knows the lake," she said more graciously. "If *you* say the steamboat is safe, Mr. Dysart, and you'll come and see we're not drowned by these harum-scarum soldiers, I've no objection to going."

Further discussion was interrupted by a rush and a scurry on the gravel of the garden path, and a flying ball of fur dashed up the outside of the window, the upper half of which was open, and suddenly realising its safety, poised itself on the sash, and crooned and spat with a collected fury at Mr. Hawkins' bull terrier, who leaped unavailingly below.

"Oh! me poor darling Bruffy!" screamed Miss Mullen, springing up and upsetting her cup of tea; "she'll be killed! Call off your dog, Mr. Hawkins!"

As if in answer to her call, a tall figure darkened the window, and Mr. Lambert pushed Mrs. Bruff into the room with the handle of his walking-stick.

"Hullo, Charlotte! Isn't that Hawkins' dog?" he began, putting his head in at the window, then, with a sudden change of manner as he caught sight of Miss Mullen's guests, "oh—I had no idea you had anyone here," he said, taking off his hat to as much of Pamela and Miss Hope-Drummond as was not hidden by Charlotte's bulky person, " I only thought I'd call round and see if Francie would like to come out for a row before dinner."

CHAPTER X.

WASHERWOMEN do not, as a rule, assimilate the principles of their trade. In Lismoyle, the row of cottages most affected by ladies of that profession was, indeed, planted by the side of the lake, but except in winter, when the floods sent a muddy wash in at the kitchen doors of Ferry Row, the customers' linen alone had any experience of its waters. The clouds of steam from the cauldrons of boiling clothes ascended from morning till night, and hung in beads upon the sooty cobwebs that draped the rafters; the food and wearing apparel of the laundresses and their vast families mingled horribly with their professional apparatus, and, outside in the road, the filthy children played among puddles that stagnated under an iridescent scum of soap-suds. A narrow strip of goose-nibbled grass divided the road from the lake shore, and at almost any hour of the day there might be seen a slatternly woman or two kneeling by the water's edge, pounding the wet linen on a rock with a flat wooden weapon, according to the immemorial custom of their savage class.

The Row ended at the ferry pier, and perhaps one reason for the absence of self-respect in the appearance of its inhabitants lay in the fact that the only passers-by were the country people on their way to the ferry, which here, where the lake narrowed to something less than a mile, was the route to the Lismoyle market generally used by the dwellers on the opposite side. The coming of a donkey-cart down the Row was an event to be celebrated, with hooting and stone-throwing by the children, and, therefore, it can be understood that when, on a certain still, sleepy afternoon Miss Mullen drove slowly in her phaeton along the line of houses, she created nearly as great a sensation as she would have made in Piccadilly.

Miss Mullen had one or two sources of income which few people knew of, and about which, with all her loud candour, she did not enlighten even

her most intimate friends. Even Mr. Lambert
might have been surprised to know that two or
three householders in Ferry Row paid rent to her,
and that others of them had money dealings with
her of a complicated kind, not easy to describe,
but simple enough to the strong financial intellect
of his predecessor's daughter. No account books
were taken with her on these occasions. She and
her clients were equally equipped with the absolutely
accurate business memory of the Irish peasant, a
memory that in few cases survives education, but,
where it exists, may be relied upon more
than all the generations of ledgers and account
books.

Charlotte's visits to Ferry Row were usually made
on foot, and were of long duration, but her business
on this afternoon was of a trivial character, consisting
merely in leaving a parcel at the house of Dinny
Crimeen, the tailor, and of convincing her washerwoman of iniquity in a manner that brought every
other washerwoman to her door, and made each offer
up thanks to her most favoured saint that she was
not employed by Miss Mullen.

The long phaeton was at last turned, with drag-
gings at the horse's mouth and grindings of the fore-
carriage ; the children took their last stare, and one or
two ladies whose payments were in arrear emerged
from their back gardens and returned to their
washing-tubs. If they flattered themselves that
they had been forgotten, they were mistaken ;
Charlotte had given a glance of grim amusement at
the deserted washing-tubs, and as her old phaeton
rumbled slowly out of Ferry Row, she was com-
puting the number of customers, and the consequent
approximate income of each defaulter.

To the deep and plainly expressed chagrin of the
black horse, he was not allowed to turn in at the gate
of Tally Ho, but was urged along the road which led
to Rosemount. There again he made a protest,
but, yielding to the weighty arguments of Charlotte's
whip, he fell into his usual melancholy jog, and took
the turn to Gurthnamuckla with dull resignation.
Once steered into that lonely road, Charlotte let him
go at his own pace, and sat passive, her mouth
tightly closed, and her eyes blinking quickly as she
looked straight ahead of her with a slight furrow of

concentration on her low forehead. She had the unusual gift of thinking out in advance her line of conversation in an interview, and, which is even less usual, she had the power of keeping to it. By sheer strength of will she could force her plan of action upon other people, as a conjuror forces a card, till they came to believe it was of their own choosing ; she had done it so often that she was now confident of her skill, and she quite understood the inevitable advantage that a fixed scheme of any sort has over indefinite opposition. When the clump of trees round Gurthnamuckla rose into view, Charlotte had determined her order of battle, and was free to give her attention to outward circumstances. It was a long time since she had been out to Miss Duffy's farm, and as the stony country began to open its arms to the rich, sweet pastures, an often repressed desire asserted itself, and Charlotte heaved a sigh that was as romantic in its way as if she had been sweet and twenty, instead of tough and forty.

Julia Duffy did not come out to meet her visitor, and when Charlotte walked into the kitchen, she

found that the mistress of the house was absent, and
that three old women were squatted on the floor in
front of the fire, smoking short clay pipes, and holding converse in Irish that was punctuated with loud
sniffs and coughs. At sight of the visitor the pipes
vanished in the twinkling of an eye, and one of the
women scrambled to her feet.

"Why, Mary Holloran, what brings you here?"
said Charlotte, recognising the woman who lived in
the Rosemount gate lodge.

"It was a sore leg I have, yer honour, miss,"
whined Mary Holloran; "it's running with me now
these three weeks, and I come to thry would Miss
Duffy give me a bit o' a plashther."

"Take care it wouldn't run away with you altogether," replied Charlotte facetiously; "and where's
Miss Duffy herself?"

"She's sick, the craythure," said one of the other
women, who, having found and dusted a chair, now
offered it to Miss Mullen; "she have a wakeness like
in her head, and an impression on her heart, and
Billy Grainy came afther Peggy Roche here, the way
she'd mind her."

Peggy Roche groaned slightly, and stirred a pot of smutty gruel with an air of authority.

"Could I see her d'ye think?" asked Charlotte, sitting down and looking about her with sharp appreciation of the substantial excellence of the smoke-blackened walls and grimy woodwork. "There wouldn't be a better kitchen in the country," she thought, "if it was properly done up."

"Ye can, asthore, ye can go up," replied Peggy Roche, "but wait a while till I have the sup o' grool hated, and maybe yerself 'll take it up to herself."

"Is she eating nothing but that?" asked Charlotte, viewing the pasty compound with disgust.

"Faith, 'tis hardly she'll ate that itself." Peggy Roche rose as she spoke, and, going to the dresser, returned with a black bottle. "As for a bit o' bread, or a pratie, or the like o' that, she couldn't use it, nor let it past her shest ; with respects to ye, as soon as she'd have it shwallied it'd come up as simple and pleashant as it wint down." She lifted the little three-legged pot off its heap of hot embers, and then took the cork out of the black bottle with nimble, dirty fingers.

"What in the name of goodness is that ye have there?" demanded Charlotte hastily.

Mrs. Roche looked somewhat confused and murmured something about "a weeshy suppeen o' shperits to wet the grool."

Charlotte snatched the bottle from her, and smelled it.

"Faugh!" she said, with a guttural at the end of the word that no Saxon gullet could hope to produce; "it's potheen! that's what it is, and mighty bad potheen too. D'ye want to poison the woman?"

A loud chorus of repudiation arose from the sick-nurse and her friends.

"As for you, Peggy Roche, you're not fit to tend a pig, let alone a Christian. You'd murder this poor woman with your filthy fresh potheen, and when your own son was dying, you begrudged him the drop of spirits that'd have kept the life in him."

Peggy flung up her hands with a protesting howl.

"May God forgive ye that word, Miss Charlotte! If 'twas the blood of me arrm, I didn't begridge it to him; the Lord have mercy on him—"

"Amen! amen! You would not, asthore," groaned the other women.

"— but does'nt the world know it's mortial sin for a poor craythure to go into th' other world with the smell of dhrink on his breath!"

"It's mortal sin to be a fool," replied Miss Mullen whose medical skill had often been baffled by such winds of doctrine; "here, give me the gruel. I'll go give it to the woman before you have her murdered." She deftly emptied the pot of gruel into a bowl, and, taking the spoon out of the old woman's hand, she started on her errand of mercy.

The stairs were just outside the door, and making their dark and perilous ascent in safety, she stood still in a low passage into which two or three other doors opened. She knocked at the first of these, and, receiving no answer, turned the handle quietly and looked in. There was no furniture in it except a broken wooden bedstead; innumerable flies buzzed on the closed window, and in the slant of sunlight that fell through the dim panes was a box from which a turkey reared its red throat, and regarded her with a suspicion born, like her chickens, of long hatching.

Charlotte closed the door and noiselessly opened the next. There was nothing in the room, which was of the ordinary low-ceiled cottage type, and after a calculating look at the broken flooring and the tattered wall-paper, she went quietly out into the passage again. "Good servants' room," she said to herself, "but if she's here much longer it'll be past praying for."

If she had been in any doubt as to Miss Duffy's whereabouts, a voice from the room at the end of the little passage now settled the matter. "Is that Peggy?" it called.

Charlotte pushed boldly into the room with the bowl of gruel.

"No, Miss Duffy, me poor old friend, it's me, Charlotte Mullen," she said in her most cordial voice; "they told me below you were ill, but I thought you'd see me, and I brought your gruel up in my hand. I hope you'll like it none the less for that!"

The invalid turned her night-capped head round from the wall and looked at her visitor with astonished, bloodshot eyes. Her hatchety face was very yellow, her long nose was rather red, and her black hair thrust itself out round the soiled frill of her night-cap in dingy wisps.

" You're welcome, Miss Mullen," she said with a pitiable attempt at dignity ; " won't you take a cheer ? "

" Not till I've seen you take this," replied Charlotte, handing her the bowl of gruel with even broader *bonhommie* than before.

Julia Duffy reluctantly sat up among her blankets, conscious almost to agony of the squalor of all her surroundings, conscious even that the blankets were of the homespun, madder-dyed flannel such as the poor people use, and taking the gruel, she began to eat it in silence. She tried to prop herself in this emergency with the recollection that Charlotte Mullen's grandfather drank her grandfather's port wine under this very roof, and that it was by no fault of hers that she had sunk while Charlotte had risen, but the worn-out boots that lay on the floor where she had thrown them off, and the rags stuffed into the broken panes in the window, were facts that crowded out all consolation from bygone glories.

" Well, Miss Duffy," said Charlotte, drawing up

a chair to the bedside, and looking at her hostess with a critical eye, " I'm sorry to see you so sick ; when Billy Grainey left the milk last night he told Norry you were laid up in bed, and I thought I'd come over and see if there was anything I could do for you."

" Thank ye, Miss Mullen," replied Julia stiffly, sipping the nauseous gruel with ladylike decorum, " I have all I require here."

" Well, ye know, Miss Duffy, I wanted to see how you are," said Charlotte, slightly varying her attack ; " I'm a bit of a doctor, like yourself. Peggy Roche below told me you had what she called ' an impression on the heart,' but it looks to me more like a touch of liver."

The invalid does not exist who can resist a discussion of symptoms, and Miss Duffy's hauteur slowly thawed before Charlotte's intelligent and intimate questions. In a very short time Miss Mullen had felt her pulse, inspected her tongue, promised to send her a bottle of unfailing efficacy, and delivered an exordium on the nature and treatment of her complaint.

" But in deed and in truth," she wound up, " if you want my opinion, I'll tell you frankly that what ails you is you're just rotting away with the damp and loneliness of this place. I declare that sometimes when I'm lying awake in my bed at nights, I've thought of you out here by yourself, without an earthly creature near you if you got sick, and wondered at you. Why, my heavenly powers ! ye might die a hundred deaths before anyone would know it ! "

Miss Duffy picked up a corner of the sheet and wiped the gruel from her thin lips.

" If it comes to that, Miss Mullen," she said with some resumption of her earlier manner, " if I'm for dying I'd as soon die by myself as in company ; and as for damp, I thank God this house was built by them that didn't spare money on it, and it's as dry this minyute as what it was forty years ago."

" What ! Do you tell me the roof's sound ? " exclaimed Charlotte with genuine interest.

" I have never examined it, Miss Mullen," replied Julia coldly, " but it keeps the rain out, and I consider that suffeecient."

" Oh, I'm sure there's not a word to be said against the house," Charlotte made hasty reparation; " but, indeed, Miss Duffy, I say—and I've heard more than myself say the same thing—that a delicate woman like you has no business to live alone so far from help. The poor Archdeacon frets about it, I can tell ye. I believe he thinks Father Heffernan'll be raking ye into his fold! And I can tell ye," concluded Charlotte, with what she felt to be a certain rough pathos, " there's plenty in Lismoyle would be sorry to see your father's daughter die with the wafer in her mouth! "

" I had no idea the people in Lismoyle were so anxious about me and my affairs," said Miss Duffy. " They're very kind, but I'm able to look afther my soul without their help."

" Well, of course, everyone's soul is their own affair; but, ye know, when no one ever sees ye in your own parish church—well, right or wrong, there are plenty of fools to gab about it."

The dark bags of skin under Julia Duffy's eyes became slowly red, a signal that this thrust had home. She did not answer, and her visitor rose, and moving towards the hermetically sealed window, looked out across the lawn over Julia's domain. Her roundest and weightiest stone was still in her sling, while her eye ran over the grazing cattle in the fields.

"Is it true what I hear, that Peter Joyce has your grazing this year?" she said casually.

"It is quite true," answered Miss Duffy, a little defiantly. A liver attack does not pre-dispose its victims to answer in a Christian spirit questions that are felt to be impertinent.

"Well," returned Charlotte, still looking out of the window, with her hands deep in the pockets of her black alpaca coat, "I'm sorry for it."

"Why so?"

Julia's voice had a sharpness that was pleasant to Miss Mullen's ear.

"I can't well explain the matter to ye now," Charlotte said, turning round and looking portentously upon the sick woman, "but I have it from a sure hand that Peter Joyce is bankrupt, and will be in the courts before the year is out."

When, a short time afterwards, Julia Duffy lay

back among her madder blankets and heard the
last sound of Miss Mullen's phaeton wheels die
away along the lake road, she felt that the visit
had at least provided her with subject for meditation.

CHAPTER XI.

MR. RODERICK LAMBERT'S study window gave upon the flower garden, and consequently the high road also came within the sphere of his observations. He had been sitting at his writing-table, since luncheon - time, dealing with a variety of business, and seldom lifting his glossy black head except when some sound in the road attracted his attention. It was not his custom to work after a solid luncheon on a close afternoon, nor was it by any means becoming to his complexion when he did so ; but the second post had brought letters of an unpleasant character that required immediate attention, and the flush on his face was not wholly due to hot beef-steak pie and sherry. It was not only that several of Sir Benjamin's tenants had attended a Land League meeting the Sunday before, and that their religious director had written to inform him that they had there pledged themselves to the Plan of Campaign. That was annoying, but as the May rents were in he had no objection to their amusing themselves as they pleased during the summer; in fact, from a point of view on which Mr. Lambert dwelt as little as possible even in his own mind, a certain amount of nominal disturbance among the tenants might not come amiss. The thing that was really vexing was the crass obstinacy of his wife's trustees, who had acquainted him with the fact that they were unable to comply with her wish that some of her capital should be sold out.

It is probably hardly necessary to say that the worthy turkey hen had expressed no such desire. A feeble, "to be sure, Roderick dear; I daresay it'd be the best thing to do; but you know I don't understand such things," had been her share of the transaction, and Mr. Lambert knew that the refusal of her trustees to make the desired concession would not ruffle so much as a feather, but he wished he could be as sure of the equanimity of his coachbuilder, one of whose numerous demands for payment was lying upon the table in front of him; while others, dating back five years to the period of his marriage, lurked in the pigeon-holes of his writing-table.

Mr. Lambert, like other young gentlemen of fashion, but not of fortune, had thought that when he married a well-to-do widow, he ought to prove his power of adjusting himself to circumstances by expending her ready money in as distinguished a manner as possible. The end of the ready money had come in an absurdly short time, and, paradoxical as it may seem, it had during its brief life raised a flourishing following of bills which had in the past spring given Mr. Lambert far more trouble than he felt them to be worth, and though he had stopped the mouths of some of the more rapacious of his creditors, he had done so with extreme difficulty and at a cost that made him tremble. It was especially provoking that the coachbuilder should have threatened legal proceedings about that bill just now, when, in addition to other complications, he happened to have lost more money at the Galway races than he cared to think about, certainly more than he wished his wife and her relations to know of.

Early in the afternoon he had, with an unregarding eye, seen Charlotte drive by on her way to Gurthnamuckla; but after a couple of hours of gloomy calculation and letter-writing, the realisation that Miss Mullen was not at her house awoke in him, coupled with the idea that a little fresh air would do him good. He went out of the house, some unconfessed purpose quickening his step. He hesitated at the gate while it expanded into determination, and then he hailed his wife, whose poppy-decked garden-hat was painfully visible above the magenta blossoms of a rhododendron bush.

· "Lucy! I wouldn't be surprised if I fetched Francie Fitzpatrick over for tea. She's by herself at Tally Ho! I saw Charlotte drive by without her a little while ago."

When he reached Tally Ho he found the gate open, an offence always visited with extremest penalties by Miss Mullen, and as he walked up the drive he noticed that, besides the broad wheel-tracks of the phaeton there were several thin and devious ones, at some places interrupted by footmarks and a general appearance of a scuffle; at another heading into a lilac bush with apparent precipitancy, and at the hall-door circling endlessly and crookedly with several excursions on to the newly-mown plot of grass.

"I wonder what perambulator has been running amuck in here. Charlotte will make it hot for them, whoever they were," thought Lambert, as he stood waiting for the door to be opened, and watched through the glass of the porch-door two sleek tortoise-shell cats lapping a saucer of yellow cream in a corner of the hall. "By Jove! how snug she is in this little place. She must have a pot of money put by; more than she'd ever own up to, I'll engage!"

At this juncture the door opened, and he was confronted by Norry the Boat, with sleeves rolled above her brown elbows and stockinged feet untrammelled by boots.

"There's noan of them within," she announced before he had time to speak. "Miss Charlotte's gone dhriving to Gurthnamuckla, and Miss Francie went out a while ago."

"Which way did she go, d'ye know?"

"Musha, faith! I do *not* know what way did she go," replied Norry, her usual asperity heightened by a recent chase of Susan, who had fled to the roof of the turf-house with a mackerel snatched from the kitchen-table. "I have plinty to do besides running afther her. I heard her spakin' to one outside in the avenue, and with that she clapped the hall-doore afther her and she didn't come in since.

Lambert thought it wiser not to venture on the suggestion that Louisa might be better informed, and walked away down the avenue trying hard not to admit to himself his disappointment.

He turned towards home again in an objectless way, thoroughly thwarted, and dismally conscious that the afternoon contained for him only the prospect of having tea with his wife and finishing his letters afterwards. His step became slower and slower as he approached his own entrance gates, and he looked at his watch.

"Confound it! it's only half-past four. I can't go in yet;" then, a new idea striking him, "perhaps she went out to meet Charlotte. I declare I might as well go a bit down the road and see if they're coming back yet."

He walked for at least half a mile under the trees, whose young June leaves had already a dissipated powdering of white limestone dust, without meeting anything except a donkey with a pair of creaking paniers on its back, walking alone and discreetly at its own side of the road, as well aware as Mr. Lambert that its owner was dallying with a quart of porter at a roadside public house a mile away. The turn to Gurthnamuckla was not far off when the distant rumble of wheels became at last audible; Lambert had only time to remember angrily that, as the Tally Ho phaeton had but two seats, he had had his walk for nothing, when the bowed head and long melancholy face of the black horse came in sight, and he became aware that Charlotte was without a companion.

Her face had more colour in it than usual as

she pulled up beside him, perhaps from the heat of the afternoon and the no small exertion of flogging her steed, and her manner when she spoke was neither bluff nor hearty, but approximated more nearly to that of ordinary womankind than was its wont. Mr. Lambert noticed none of these things ; and, being a person whose breeding was not always equal to annoying emergencies, he did not trouble himself to take off his hat or smile appropriately as Charlotte said—

"Well, Roddy, I'd as soon expect to see your two horses sitting in the dog-cart driving you as to see you as far from home as this on your own legs. Where are you off to?"

"I was taking a stroll out to meet you, and ask you to come back and have tea with Lucy," replied Mr. Lambert, recognising the decree of fate with a singularly bad grace. " I went down to Tally Ho to ask you, and Norry told me you had gone to Gurth-namuckla."

" Did you see Francie there ? " said Charlotte quickly.

" No ; I believe she was out somewhere."

" Well, you were a very good man to take so much trouble about us," she replied, looking at him with an expression that softened the lines of her face in a surprising way. " Are you too proud to have a lift home now ? "

" Thank you, I'd sooner walk—and—" casting about for an excuse—" you mightn't like the smell of my cigar under your nose."

" Come, now, Roddy," exclaimed Charlotte, " you ought to know me better than that ! Don't you remember how you used to sit smoking beside me in the office when I was helping you to do your work ? In fact, I wouldn't say that there hadn't been an occasion when I was guilty of a cigarette in your company myself ! "

She turned her eyes towards him, and the provocative look in them came as instinctively and as straight as ever it did from Francie's, or as ever it has been projected from the curbed heart of woman. But, unfair as it may be, it is certain that if Lambert had seen it, he would not have been attracted by it. He, however, did not look up.

"Well, if you don't mind going slow, I'll walk beside you," he said, ignoring the reminiscence. " I want to know whether you did better business with Julia Duffy than I did last week."

The soft look was gone in a moment from Charlotte's face.

"I couldn't get much satisfaction out of her," she replied; "but I think I left a thorn in her pillow when I told her Peter Joyce was bankrupt."

"I'll take my oath you did," said Lambert, with a short laugh. "I declare I'd be sorry for the poor old devil if she wasn't such a bad tenant, letting the whole place go to the mischief, house and all."

"I tell you the house isn't in such a bad way as you think; it's dirt ails it more than anything else." Charlotte had recovered her wonted energy of utterance. "Believe me, if I had a few workmen in that house for a month you wouldn't know it."

"Well, I believe you will, sooner or later. All the same, I can't see what the deuce you want with it. Now, if *I* had the place, I'd make a pot of money out of it, keeping young horses there, as I've often told you. I'd do a bit of coping, and

making hunters to sell. There's no work on earth
I'd like as well."

He took a long pull at his cigar, and expelled a
sigh and a puff of smoke.

"Well, Roddy," said Charlotte, after a moment's
pause, speaking with an unusual slowness and
almost hesitancy, "you know I wouldn't like to
come between you and your fancy. If you want
the farm, in God's name take it yourself!"

"Take it myself! I haven't the money to pay
the fine, much less to stock it. I tell you what,
Charlotte," he went on, turning round and putting
his hand on the splash-board of the phaeton as he
walked, "you and I are old pals, and I don't mind
telling you it's the most I can do to keep going
the way I am now. I never was so driven for
money in my life," he ended, some vague purpose,
added to the habit of an earlier part of his life,
pushing him on to be confidential.

"Who's driving you, Roddy?" said Charlotte, in
a voice in which a less preoccupied person than her
companion might have noticed a curiously gentle
inflection.

It is perhaps noteworthy that while Mr. Lambert's lips replied with heartfelt irritation, " Oh, they're all at me, Langford the coachbuilder, and everyone of them," one section of his brain was asking the other how much ready money old Mrs. Mullen had had to leave, and was receiving a satisfactory answer.

There was a pause in the conversation. It was so long now since the black horse had felt the whip, that, acting on the presumption that his mistress had fallen asleep, he fell into an even more slumbrous crawl without any notice being taken.

" Roddy," said Charlotte at last, and Lambert now observed how low and rough her voice was, " do you remember in old times once or twice, when you were put to it for a five-pound note, you made no bones about asking a friend to help you? Well, you know I'm a poor woman "—even at this moment Charlotte's caution asserted itself—" but I daresay I could put my hand on a couple of hundred, and if they'd be any use to you ——"

Lambert became very red. The possibility of some such climax as this had floated in a sub-current of thought just below the level of formed ideas, but now that it had come, it startled him. It was an unheard-of thing that Charlotte should make such an offer as this. It gave him suddenly a tingling sense of power, and at the same time a strange instinct of disgust and shame.

"Oh, my dear Charlotte," he began awkwardly, "upon my soul you're a great deal too good. I never thought of such a thing—I—I—" he stammered, wishing he could refuse, but casting about for words in which to accept.

"Ah, nonsense. Now, Roddy, me dear boy," interrupted Charlotte, regaining her usual manner as she saw his embarrassment, "say no more about it. We'll consider it a settled thing, and we'll go through the base business details after tea."

Lambert said to himself that there was really no way out of it. If she was so determined the only thing was to let her do as she liked ; no one could say that the affair was of his seeking.

"And, you know," continued Charlotte in her most jocular voice, before he could frame a sentence of the right sort, "who knows, if I get the farm, that we mightn't make a joint-stock business out of it, and have young horses there, and all the rest of it!"

"You're awfully good, Charlotte," said Lambert, with an emotion in his voice that she did not guess to be purely the result of inward relief and exultation; "I'm awfully obliged to you—you always were a—a true friend—some day, perhaps, I'll be able to show you what I think about it," he stammered, unable to think of anything else to say, and, lifting his hand from the splash-board, he put it on hers, that lay in her lap with the reins in it, and pressed it for a moment. Into both their minds shot simultaneously the remembrance of a somewhat similar scene, when, long ago, Charlotte had come to the help of her father's pupil, and he had expressed his gratitude in a more ardent manner —a manner that had seemed cheap enough to him at the time, but that had been more costly to Charlotte than any other thing that had ever befallen her.

"You haven't forgotten old times any more than I have," he went on, knowing very well that he was taking now much the same

simple and tempting method of getting rid of his
obligation that he had once found so efficacious,
and to a certain extent enjoying the thought that
he could still make a fool of her. "Ah, well!"
he sighed, "there's no use trying to get those
times back, any more than there is in trying to
forget them." He hesitated. "But, after all, there's
many a new tune played on an old fiddle! Isn't that
so?" He was almost frightened at his own daring as he saw Charlotte's cheek burn with a furious
red, and her lips quiver in the attempt to answer.

Upon their silence there broke from the distance a
loud scream, then another, and then a burst of laughter in a duet of soprano and bass, coming apparently
from a lane that led into the road a little further on—
a smooth and secluded little lane, bordered thickly
with hazel bushes—a private road, in fact, to a
model farm that Mr. Lambert had established on
his employer's property. From the mouth of this
there broke suddenly a whirling vision of white-
ness and wheels, and Miss Fitzpatrick, mounted on
a tricycle and shrieking loudly, dashed across the
high road and collapsed in a heap in the ditch.

Lambert started forward, but long before he could reach her the Rev. Joseph Corkran emerged at full speed from the lane, hatless, with long flying coat-tails, and, with a skill born of experience, extricated Francie from her difficulties.

"Oh, I'm dead!" she panted. "Oh, the horrible thing! What good were you that you let it go?" unworthily attacking the equally exhausted Corkran. Then, in tones of consternation, "Goodness! Look at Mr. Lambert and Charlotte! Oh, Mr. Lambert," as Lambert came up to her, "did you see the toss I got? The dirty thing ran away with me down the hill, and Mr. Corkran was so tired running he had to let go, and I declare I thought I was killed— and you don't look a bit sorry for me!"

"Well, what business had you to get up on a thing like that?" answered Lambert, looking angrily at the curate. "I wonder, Corkran, you hadn't more sense than to let a lady ride that machine."

"Well, indeed, Mr. Lambert, I told Miss Fitzpatrick it wasn't as easy as she thought," replied the guilty Corkran, a callow youth from Trinity

College, Dublin, who had been as wax in Francie's
hands, and who now saw, with unfeigned terror,
the approach of Charlotte. " I begged of her not
to go outside Tally Ho, but—but—I think I'd
better go back and look for my hat—" he ended
abruptly, retreating into the lane just as Charlotte
drew up the black horse and opened her mouth to
deliver herself of her indignation.

CHAPTER XII.

THE broad limestone steps at Bruff looked across the lawn to the lake, and to the south. They were flanked on either hand by stone balustrades which began and ended in a pot of blazing scarlet geraniums, and on their topmost plateau on this brilliant 1st of July, the four Bruff dogs sat on their haunches and gazed with anxious despondency in at the open hall-door. For the last half-hour Max and Dinah, the indoor dogs, had known that an expedition was toward. They had seen Pamela put on a hat that certainly was not her garden one, and as certainly lacked the veil that betokened the abhorred ceremony of church-going. They knew this hat well, and at the worst it usually meant a choir practice; but taken in connection with a blue serge skirt and the packing of a luncheon basket, they almost ventured to hope it

167

portended a picnic on the lake. They adored pic-
nics. In the first place, the outdoor dogs were
always left at home, which alone would have im-
parted a delicious flavour to any entertainment,
and in the second, all dietary rules were remitted
for the occasion, and they were permitted to raven
unchecked upon chicken bones, fat slices of ham,
and luscious leavings of cream when the packing-
up time came. There was, however, mingled
with this enchanting prospect, the fear that
they might be left behind, and from the sounding
of the first note of preparation they had never
let Pamela out of their sight. Whenever her step
was heard through the long passages there had
gone with it the scurrying gallop of the two little
waiters on providence, and when her arrangements
had culminated in the luncheon basket their agitation had become so poignant that a growling game
of play under the table, got up merely to pass the
time, turned into an acrimonious squabble, and
caused their ejection to the hall-door steps by
Lady Dysart. Now, sitting outside the door, they
listened with trembling to the discussion that was

going on in the hall, and with the self-conscious-
ness of dogs were convinced that it was all about
themselves.

"No, I cannot allow Garry to go," declaimed
Lady Dysart, her eyes raised to the ceiling as if
to show her remoteness from all human entreaty;
"he is *not* over the whooping-cough; I heard him
whooping this morning in his bedroom."

The person mentioned ceased from a game of
fives with a tennis-ball that threatened moment-
arily to break the windows, and said indignantly,
"Oh, I say, mother, that was only the men in the
yard pumping. That old pump makes a row just
like whooping-cough."

Lady Dysart faltered for a moment before this
ingenious falsehood, but soon recovered herself.

"I don't care whether it was you or the pump
that whooped, it does not alter the fact of your
superfluity at a picnic."

"I think Captain Cursiter and Mr. Hawkins
wanted him to stoke," said Pamela from the
luncheon basket.

"I have no doubt they do, but they shall not

have him," said Lady Dysart with the blandness of entire decision, though her eyes wavered from her daughter's face to her son's; "they're very glad indeed to save their own clothes and spoil his."

"Well, then, I'll go with Lambert," said Garry rebelliously.

"You will do nothing of the sort!" exclaimed Lady Dysart, "whatever I may do about allowing you to go with Captain Cursiter, nothing shall induce me to sanction any plan that involves your going in that most dangerous yacht. Christopher himself says she is over-sparred." Lady Dysart had no idea of the meaning of the accusation, but she felt the term to be good and telling. "Now, Pamela, will you promise me to stay with Captain Cursiter all the time?"

"Oh, yes, I will," said Pamela laughing; "but you know in your heart that he would much rather have Garry."

"I don't care what my heart knows," replied Lady Dysart magnificently, "I know what my mouth says, and that is that you must neither of you stir out of the steam-launch."

At this descent of his mother into the pit so artfully digged for her, Garry withdrew to attire himself for the position of stoker, and Pamela discreetly changed the conversation.

It seemed a long time to Max and Dinah before their fate was decided, but after some last moments of anguish on the pier they found themselves, the one coiled determinedly on Pamela's lap, and the other smirking in the bow in Garry's arms, as Mr. Hawkins sculled the second relay of the Bruff party out to the launch. The first relay, consisting of Christopher and Miss Hope - Drummond, was already on its way down the lake in Mr. Lambert's 5-ton boat, with every inch of canvas set to catch the light and shifty breeze that blew petulantly down from the mountains, and ruffled the glitter of the lake with dark blue smears. The air quivered hotly over the great stones on the shore, drawing out the strong aromatic smell of the damp weeds and the bog-myrtle, and Lady Dysart stood on the end of the pier, and wrung her hands as she thought of Pamela's complexion.

Captain Cursiter was one of the anomalous
soldiers whose happiness it is to spend as much
time as possible in a boat, dressed in disreput-
able clothes, with hands begrimed and blistered
with oil or ropes as the case may be, and steaming or sailing to nowhere and back again with un-
dying enthusiasm. He was a thin, brown man,
with a moustache rather lighter in colour than the
tan of his face, and his beaky nose, combined with
his disposition to flee from the haunts of men, had
inspired his friends to bestow on .him the pet name
of "Snipey." The festivity on which he was at
present embarked was none of his seeking, and it
had been only by strenuous argument, fortified by
the artful suggestion that no one else was really
competent to work the boat, that Mr. Hawkins
had got him into clean flannels and the conduct
of the expedition. He knew neither Miss Mullen
nor Francie, and his acquaintance with the Dysarts,
as with other dwellers in the neighbourhood, was
of a slight and unprogressive character, and in
strong contrast to the manner in which Mr.
Hawkins had become at Bruff and elsewhere what

that young gentleman was pleased to term "the gated infant." During the run from Lismoyle to Bruff he had been able to occupy himself with the affairs of the steam-launch; but when Hawkins, his prop and stay, had rowed ashore for the Dysart party, the iron had entered into his soul.

As the punt neared the launch, Mr. Hawkins looked round to take his distance in bringing her alongside, and recognised with one delighted glance the set smile of suffering politeness that denoted that Captain Cursiter was making himself agreeable to the ladies. Charlotte was sitting in the stern with a depressing air of Sunday-outness about her, and a stout umbrella over her head. It was not in her nature to feel shy; the grain of it was too coarse and strong to harbour such a thing as diffidence, but she knew well enough when she was socially unsuccessful, and she was already aware that she was going to be out of her element on this expe-dition. Lambert, who would have been a kind of connecting link, was already far in the offing. Captain Cursiter she mentally characterised as a

poor stick. Hawkins, whom she had begun by
liking, was daily—almost hourly—gaining in her
disfavour, and from neither Pamela, Francie, or
Garry did she expect much entertainment. Charlotte had a vigorous taste in conversation, and her
idea of a pleasure party was not to talk to Pamela
Dysart about the choir and the machinery of a
school feast for an hour and a half, and from time
to time to repulse with ill-assumed politeness the
bird-like flights of Dinah on to her lap. Francie
and Mr. Hawkins sat forward on the roof of the
little cabin, and apparently entertained one another
vastly, judging by their appearance and the fragments of conversation that from time to time made
their way aft in the environment of a cloud of
smuts. Captain Cursiter, revelling in the well-
known restrictions that encompass the man at the
wheel, stood serenely aloof, steering among the
hump-backed green islands and treacherous shal-
lows, and thinking to himself that Hawkins was
going ahead pretty fast with that Dublin girl.

Mr. Hawkins had been for some time a source
of anxiety to his brother officers, who disapproved

of matrimony for the young of their regiment. Things had looked so serious when he was quartered at Limerick that he had been hurriedly sent on detachment to Lismoyle before he had time to "make an example of himself," as one of the most unmarried of the majors observed, and into Captain Cursiter's trusted hands he had been committed, with urgent instructions to keep an eye on him. Cursiter's eye was renowned for its blighting qualities on occasions such as these, and his jibes at matrimony were looked on by his brother officers as the most finished and scathing expressions of proper feeling on the subject that could be desired; but it was agreed that he would have his hands full.

The launch slid smoothly along with a low clicking of the machinery, cutting her way across the reflections of the mountains in pursuit of the tall, white sail of the *Daphne*, that seemed each moment to grow taller, as the yacht was steadily overhauled by her more practical comrade. The lake was narrower here, where it neared the end of its twenty-mile span, and so calm that the sheep and cattle grazing on the brown mountains were reflected in its depths, and the yacht seemed as incongruous in the midst of them as the ark on Mount Ararat.   The last bend of the lake was before them ; the *Daphne* crept round it, moved mysteriously by a wind that was imperceptible to the baking company on the steam-launch, and by the time the latter had churned her way round the fir-clad point, the yacht was letting go her anchor near the landing-place of a large wooded island.

At a picnic nothing is of much account before luncheon, and the gloom of hunger hung like a pall over the party that took ashore luncheon baskets, unpacked knives and forks, and gathered stones to put on the corners of the table-cloth. But such a hunger is Nature's salve for the inadequacy of human beings to amuse themselves ; the body comes to the relief of the mind with the compassionate superiority of a good servant, and confers inward festivity upon many a dull dinner party.   Max and Dinah were quite of this opinion. They had behaved with commendable fortitude during the voyage, though in the earlier part of it a shuddering dejection on Max's part had seemed to Pamela's trained eye to forbode sea-sickness, but at the lifting of the luncheon basket into the punt their self-control deserted them. The succulent trail left upon the air, palpable to the dog-nose as the smoke of the steam-launch to the human eye, beguiled them into efforts to follow, which were only suppressed by their being secretly immured in the cabin by Garry. No one but he saw the two wan faces that yearned at the tiny cabin windows, as the last punt load left for the land, and when at last the wails of the captives streamed across the water, anyone but Garry would have repented of the cruelty. The dogs will never forget it to Captain Cursiter that it was he who rowed out to the launch and brought them ashore to enjoy their fair share of the picnic, and their gratitude will never be tempered by the knowledge that he had caught at the excuse to escape from the conversation which Miss Hope-Drummond, notwithstanding even the pangs of hunger, was proffering to him.

There is something unavoidably vulgar in the

aspect of a picnic party when engaged in the culminating rite of eating on the grass. They may
feel themselves to be picturesque, gipsy-like, even
romantic, but to the unparticipating looker-on, not
even the gilded dignity of champagne can redeem
them from being a mere group of greedy, huddled backs, with ugly trimmings of paper, dirty
plates, and empty bottles. But at Innishochery the
only passers-by were straight-flying wild-duck or
wood-pigeons, or an occasional sea-gull lounging
up from the distant Atlantic, all observant enough
in their way, but not critical. It is probable they
did not notice even the singular ungracefulness of
Miss Mullen's attitude, as she sat with her short
legs uncomfortably tucked away, and her large
jaws moving steadily as she indemnified herself
for the stupidity of the recent trip. The champagne at length had its usual beneficent effect upon
the conversation. Charlotte began to tell stories
about her cats and her servants to Christopher
and Pamela, with admirable dramatic effect and a
sense of humour that made her almost attractive.
Miss Hope-Drummond had discovered that Cursi-

ter was one of the Lincolnshire Cursiters, and,
with mutual friends as stepping-stones, was working
her way on with much ability; and Francie was
sitting on a mossy rock, a little away from the
table-cloth, with a plate of cherry-pie on her lap,
Mr. Hawkins at her feet, and unlimited oppor-
tunities for practical jestings with the cherry-stones.
Garry and the dogs were engaged in scraping
out dishes and polishing plates in a silence more
eloquent than words; Lambert alone, of all the
party, remained impervious to the influences of
luncheon, and lay on his side with his eyes
moodily fixed upon his plate, only responding to
Miss Mullen's frequent references to him by a
sarcastic grunt.

"Now I assure you, Miss Dysart, it's perfectly
true," said Charlotte, after one of these polite re-
joinders. "He's too lazy to say so, but he knows
right well that when I complained of my kitchen-
maid to her mother, all the good I got from her
was that she said, 'Would ye be agin havin' a
switch and to be switchin' her!' That was a
pretty way for me to spend my valuable time." '

Her audience laughed; and inspired by another half glass of champagne, Miss Mullen continued, "But big a fool as Bid Sal is, she's a Solon beside Donovan.   He came to me th' other day and said he wanted 'little Johanna for the garden.' 'Little *who?*' says I; 'Little Johanna,' says he.   'Ye great, lazy fool,' says I, 'aren't ye big enough and ugly enough to do that little pick of work by yerself without wanting a girl to help ye?' And after all," said Charlotte, dropping from the tones of fury in which she had rendered her own part in the interview, "all he wanted was some guano for my early potatoes!"

Lambert got up without a smile, and sauntering down to the lake, sat down on a rock and began to smoke a cigar.   He could not laugh as Christopher and even Captain Cursiter did, at Charlotte's dramatisation of her scene with her gardener.   At an earlier period of his career he had found her conversation amusing, and he had not thought her vulgar.   Since then he had raised himself just high enough from the sloughs of Irish middle-class society to see its vulgarity, but he did not stand sufficiently apart from it to be able to appreciate its humorous side, and in any case he was at present little disposed to laugh at anything. He sat and smoked morosely for some time, feeling that he was making his dissatisfaction with the entertainment imposingly conspicuous; but his cigar was a failure, the rock was far from comfortable, and his bereaved friends seemed to be enjoying themselves rather more than when he left them. He threw the cigar into the water in front of him, to the consternation of a number of minnows, who had hung in the warm shallow as if listening, and now vanished in a twinkling to spread among the dark resorts of the elder fishes the tale of the thunderbolt that fell in their midst, while Lambert stalked back to the party under the trees.

Its component parts were little altered, saving that Miss Hope-Drummond had, by the ingenious erection of a parasol, isolated herself and Christopher from the others, and that Garry had joined himself to Francie and Hawkins, and was, in company with the latter, engaged in weaving stalks of grass across the insteps of Miss Fitzpatrick's open-worked stockings.

"Just look at them, Mr. Lambert," Francie called out in cheerful complaint. "They're having a race to see which of them will finish their bit of grass first, and they won't let me stir, though I'm nearly mad with the flies!"

She had a waving branch of mountain-ash in her hand ; the big straw hat that she had trimmed for herself with dog-roses the night before was on the back of her head ; her hair clustered about her white temples, and the colour that fighting the flies had brought to her face lent a lovely depth to eyes that had the gaiety and the soullessness of a child. Lambert had forgotten most of his classics since he had left school, and it is probable that even had he remembered them it would not have occurred to him to regard anything in them as applicable to modern times. At all events Francie's Dryad-like fitness to her surroundings did not strike him, as it struck another more dispassionate onlooker, when an occasional lift of the Hope-Drummond parasol revealed the white-clad finger with its woody background to Christopher.

"It seems to me you're very well able to take care of yourself," was Lambert's reply to Miss Fitzpatrick's appeal. He turned his back upon her, and interrupted Charlotte in the middle of a story by asking her if she would walk with him across the island and have a look at the ruins ot Ochery Chapel.

One habit at least of Mr. Lambert's school life remained with him. He was still a proficient at telling tales.

CHAPTER XIII.

INNISHOCHERY ISLAND lay on the water like a great green bouquet, with a narrow grey lace edging of stony beach. From the lake it seemed that the foliage stood in a solid impenetrable mass, and that nothing but the innumerable wood-pigeons could hope to gain its inner recesses; even the space of grass which, at the side of the landing-place, drove a slender wedge up among the trees, had still the moss-grown stumps upon it that told it had been recovered by force from the possession of the tall pines and thick hazel and birch scrub. The end of the wedge narrowed into a thread of a path which wound its briary way among the trees with such sinuous vagueness, and such indifference to branches overhead and rocks underfoot, that to follow it was both an act of faith and a penance. Near the middle of the island it was interrupted by a brook that slipped along whispering to itself through the silence of the wood, and though the path made a poor shift to maintain its continuity with stepping-stones, it expired a few paces farther on in the bracken of a little glade.

It was a glade that had in some elfish way acquired an expression of extremest old age. The moss grew deep in the grass, lay deep on the rocks; stunted birch-trees encircled it with pale twisted arms hoary with lichen, and, at the farther end of it, a grey ruined chapel, standing over the pool that was the birthplace of the stream, fulfilled the last requirement of romance. On this hot summer afternoon the glade had more than ever its air of tranced meditation upon other days and superiority to the outer world, lulled in its sovereignty of the island by the monotone of humming insects, while on the topmost stone of the chapel a magpie gabbled and cackled like a court jester. Christopher thought, as he sat by the pool smoking a cigarette, that he had done well in staying behind under the pretence of photographing the yacht from the landing-place, and thus eluding the rest of the party. He was only intermittently unsociable, but he had always had a taste for his own society, and, as he said to himself, he had been going strong all the morning, and the time had come for solitude and tobacco.

He was a young man of a reflective turn, and had artistic aspirations which, had he been of a hardier nature, would probably have taken him further than photography. But Christopher's temperament held one or two things unusual in the amateur. He had the saving, or perhaps fatal power of seeing his own handiwork with as unflattering an eye as he saw other people's. He had no confidence in anything about himself except his critical ability, and as he did not satisfy that, his tentative essays in painting died an early death. It was the same with everything else. His fastidious dislike of doing a thing indifferently was probably a form of conceit, and though it was a higher form than the common vanity whose geese are all swans, it brought about in him a kind of deadlock. His relations thought him extremely clever, on the strength of his university career and his intellectual fastidiousness, and he himself was aware that he was clever, and cared very little for the knowledge. Half the people in the world were clever nowadays, he said to himself with indolent irritability, but genius was another affair; and, having torn up his latest efforts in water-colour and verse, he bought a camera, and betook himself to the more attainable perfection of photography.

It was delightful to lie here with the delicate cigarette smoke keeping the flies at bay, and the grasshoppers whirring away in the grass, like fairy sewing-machines, and with the soothing knowledge that the others had been through the glade, had presumably done the ruin thoroughly, and were now cutting their boots to pieces on the water-fretted limestone rocks as they scrambled round from the shore to the landing-place. This small venerable wood, and the boulders that had lain about the glade through sleepy centuries till the moss had smothered their outlines, brought to Christopher's mind the enchanted country through which King Arthur's knights rode; and he lay there mouthing to himself fragments of half-remembered verse, and wondering at the chance that had reserved for him this backwater in a day of otherwise dubious enjoyment. He even found himself piecing together a rhyme or two on his own account ; but, as is often the case, inspiration was paralysed by the overwhelming fulness of the reality ; the fifth line refused to express his idea, and the interruption of lyric emotion caused by the making and lighting of a fresh cigarette proved fatal to the prospects of the sonnet. He felt disgusted with himself and his own futility. When he had been at Oxford not thus had the springs of inspiration ceased to flow. He had begun to pass the period of water-colours then, but not the period when ideas are as plenty and as full of novelty as leaves in spring, and the knowledge has not yet come that they, like the leaves, are old as the world itself.

For the past three or four years the social exigencies of Government House life had not proved conducive to fervour of any kind, and now, while he was dawdling away his time at Bruff, in the uninterested expectation of another appointment,

he found that he not only could not write,
but that he seemed to have lost the wish to
try.

"I suppose I am sinking into the usual bucolic
stupor," he said to himself, as he abandoned the
search for the vagrant rhyme. "If I only could
read the *Field*, and had a more spontaneous
habit of cursing, I should be an ideal country
gentleman."

He crumpled into his pocket again the envelope on
the back of which he had been scribbling, and told
himself that it was more philosophic and more
simple to enjoy things in the homely, pre-historic
manner, without trying to express them elaborately
for the benefit of others. He was intellectually
effete, and what made his effeteness more hopeless
was that he recognised it himself. "I am perfectly
happy if I let myself alone," was the sum of his
reflections. "They gave me a little more culture
than I could hold, and it ran over the edge at first.
Now I think I'm just about sufficiently up in the
bottle for Lismoyle form." He tilted his straw hat
over his nose, shut his eyes, and, leaning back, soon

felt the delicious fusion into his brain of the sur-
rounding hum and soft movement that tells of the
coming of out-of-door summer sleep.

It is deplorable to think of what figure Christopher
must cut in the eyes of those whose robuster taste
demands in a young man some more potent and
heroic qualities, a gentlemanly hardihood in language
and liquor, an interesting suggestion of moral
obliquity, or, at least, some hereditary vice on which
the character may make shipwreck with magnificent
helplessness.   Christopher, with his preference for
his sister's society, and his lack of interest in the
majority of manly occupations, from hunting to
music halls, has small claim to respect or admiration.
The invertebrateness of his character seemed to be
expressed in his attitude, as he lay, supine, under
the birch trees, with the grass making a luxurious
couch for his lazy limbs, and the faint breeze just
stirring about him.   His sleep was not deep enough
to still the breath of summer in his ears, but it had
quieted the jabber of the magpie to a distant purring,
and he was fast falling into the abyss of unconsciousness, when a gentle, regular sound made itself felt,

the fall of a footstep and the brushing of a skirt
through the grass. He lay very still, and cherished
an ungenial hope that the white-stemmed birches
might mercifully screen him from the invader.
The step came nearer, and something in its solidity
and determination gave Christopher a guess as to
whose it was, that was speedily made certainty by a
call that jarred all the sleepy enchantment of the
glade.

" Fran-cie ! "

Christopher shrank lower behind a mossy stone,
and wildly hoped that his unconcealable white
flannels might be mistaken for the stem of a fallen
birch.

" Fran-cie ! "

It had come nearer, and Christopher anticipated
the inevitable discovery by getting up and speaking.

" I'm afraid she's not here, Miss Mullen. She
has not been here for half an hour at least."
He did not feel bound to add that when he
first sat down by the pool, he had heard Miss
Fitzpatrick's and Mr. Hawkins' voices in high
and agreeable altercation on the opposite side of

the island to that taken by the rest of the party.

The asperity that had been discernible in Miss Mullen's summons to her cousin vanished at once.

"My goodness me! Mr. Dysart! To think of your being here all the time, 'Far from the madding crowd's ignoble strife!' Here I am hunting for that naughty girl to tell her to come and help to make tea, instead of letting your poor sister have all the trouble by herself."

Charlotte was rather out of breath, and looked hot and annoyed, in spite of the smile with which she lubricated her remark.

"Oh, my sister is used to that sort of thing," said Christopher, "and Miss Hope-Drummond is there to help, isn't she?"

Charlotte had seated herself on a rock, and was fanning herself with her pocket-handkerchief; evidently going to make herself agreeable, Christopher thought, with an irritability that lost no detail of her hand's ungainly action.

"I don't think Miss Hope-Drummond is much in the utilitarian line," she said, with a laugh that was as slighting as she dared to make it. "Hers is the purely ornamental, I should imagine. Now, I will say for poor Francie, if she was there, no one would work harder than she would, and, though I say it that shouldn't, I think she's ornamental too."

"Oh, highly ornamental," said Christopher politely. "I don't think there can be any doubt about that."

"You're very good to say so," replied Charlotte effusively; "but I can tell you, Mr. Dysart, that poor child has had to make herself useful as well as ornamental before now. From what she tells me I suspect there were few things she didn't have to put her hand to before she came down to me here."

"Really!" said Christopher, as politely as before, "that was very hard luck."

"You may say that it was!" returned Charlotte, planting a hand on each knee with elbows squared outwards, as was her wont in moments of excitement, and taking up her parable against the Fitz-patricks with all the enthusiasm of a near relation. "Her uncle and aunt are very good people in their way, I suppose, but beyond feeding her and putting clothes on her back, I don't know what they did for her."

Charlotte had begun her sentence with comparative calm, but she had gathered heat and velocity as she proceeded. She paused with a snort, and Christopher, who had never before been privileged to behold her in her intenser moments, said, without a very distinct idea of what was expected of him :

" Oh, really, and who are these amiable people ? "

" Fitzpatricks ! " spluttered Miss Mullen, " and no better than the dirt under my poor cousin Isabella Mullen's feet. It's through *her* Francie's related to me, and not through the Fitzpatricks at all. *I'm* no relation of the Fitzpatricks, thank God ! My father's brother married a Butler, and Francie's grandmother was a Butler too— "

" It's very intricate," murmured Christopher ; " it sounds as if she ought to have been a parlour-maid."

" And that's the only connection I am of the Fitzpatricks," continued Miss Mullen at lightning speed, oblivious of interruption ; " but Francie takes after her mother's family and her grandmother's family, and your poor father would tell you if he was able, that the Butlers of Tally Ho were as well known in their time as the Dysarts of Bruff!"

"I'm sure he would," said Christopher feebly, thinking as he spoke that his conversations with his father had been wont to treat of more stirring and personal topics than the bygone glories of the Butlers.

"Yes, indeed, as good a family as any in the county. People laugh at me, and say I'm mad about family and pedigree; but I declare to goodness, Mr. Dysart, I think the French are right when they say, '*bong song ne poo mongtir*,' and there's nothing like good blood after all."

Charlotte possessed the happy quality of believing in the purity of her own French accent, and she felt a great satisfaction in rounding her peroration with a quotation in that tongue. She had, moreover, worked off some of the irritation which had, from various causes, been seething within her when she met Christopher; and when she resumed her discourse it was in the voice of the orator, who, having ranted out one branch of his subject, enters upon the next with almost awful quietness.

" I don't know why I should bore you about a purely family matter, Mr. Dysart, but the truth is, it cuts me to the heart when I see your sister— your charming sister—yes, and Miss Hope-Drum- mond too—not that I'd mention her in the same breath with Miss Dysart—with every advantage that education can give them, and then to think of that poor girl, brought up from hand to mouth, and her little fortune that should have been spent on herself going, as I may say, to fill the stomachs of the Fitzpatricks' brood ! "

Christopher raised himself from the position of leaning against a tree, in which he had listened, not without interest, to the recital of Francie's wrongs.

" I don't think you need apologise for Miss Fitz- patrick," he said, rather more coldly than he had yet spoken. He had ceased to be amused by Miss Mullen ; eccentricity was one thing, but vulgar want of reserve was another; he wondered if she discussed her cousin's affairs thus openly with all his friends.

" It's very kind of you to say so," rejoined Miss Mullen eagerly," but I know very well you're not blind, any more than I am, and all my affection for the girl can't make me shut my eyes to what's unlady-like or bad style, though I know it's not her fault."

Christopher looked at his watch surreptitiously.

" Now I'm delaying you in a most unwarrantable way," said Charlotte, noting and interpreting the action at once, " but I got so hot and tired running about the woods that I had to take a rest. I was trying to get a chance to say a word to your sister about Francie to ask her to be kind to her, but I daresay it'll come to the same thing now that I've had a chat with you," she concluded, rising from her seat and smiling with luscious affability.

A little below the pond two great rocks leaned towards each other, and between them a hawthorn bush had pressed itself up to the light. Something like a path was trodden round the rocks, and a few rags impaled on the spikes of the thorn bush denoted that it marked the place of a holy

well. Conspicuous among these votive offerings
were two white rags, new and spotless, and altogether out of keeping with the scraps of red
flannel and dirty frieze that had been left by the
faithful in lieu of visiting cards for the patron
saint of the shrine. Christopher and Charlotte's
way led them within a few yards of the spot; the
latter's curiosity induced her, as she passed, to
examine the last contributions to the thorn bush.

"I wonder who has been tearing up their best
pocket-handkerchiefs for a wish?" said Christopher,
putting up his eye-glass and peering at the rags.

"Two bigger fools than the rest of them, I suppose," said Miss Mullen shortly; "we'd better hurry
on now, Mr. Dysart, or we'll get no tea."

She swept Christopher in front of her along the
narrow path before he had time to see that the
last two pilgrims had determined that the saint
should make no mistake about their identity, and
had struck upon the thorn bush the corners of
their handkerchiefs, one of them, a silken triangle,
having on it the initials G.H., while on the other
was a large and evidently home-embroidered F.

CHAPTER XIV.

LATE that afternoon, when the sun was beginning to stoop to the west, a wind came creeping down from somewhere back of the mountains, and began to stretch tentative cats' paws over the lake. It had pushed before it across the Atlantic a soft mass of orange-coloured cloud, that caught the sun's lowered rays, and spread them in a mellow glare over everything. The lake turned to a coarse and furious blue; all the rocks and tree stems became like red gold, and the polished brass top of the funnel of the steam-launch looked as if it were on fire as Captain Cursiter turned the *Serpolette's* sharp snout to the wind, and steamed at full speed round Ochery Point. The yacht had started half an hour before on her tedious zig-zag journey home, and was already far down to the right, her sails all aglow as she leaned aslant like a skater, swooping and bending under the freshening breeze.

It was evident that Lambert wished to make the most of his time, for almost immediately after the *Daphne* had gone about with smooth precision, and had sprung away on the other tack, the party on the launch saw a flutter of white, and a top-sail was run up.

"By Jove! Lambert didn't make much on that tack," remarked Captain Cursiter to his brother-in-arms, as with an imperceptible pressure of the wheel he serenely headed the launch straight for her destination, "I don't believe he's done himself much good with that top-sail either."

Mr. Hawkins turned a sour eye upon the *Daphne* and said laconically, "Silly ass; he'll smother her."

"Upon my word, I don't think he'll get in much before nine o'clock to-night," continued Cursiter; "it's pretty nearly dead in his teeth, and he doesn't make a hundred yards on each tack."

Mr. Hawkins slammed the lid of the coal-bunker, and stepped past his chief into the after-part of the launch.

"I say, Miss Mullen," he began with scarcely suppressed malignity, "Captain Cursiter says you won't see your niece before to-morrow morning. You'll be sorry you wouldn't let her come home in the launch after all."

"If she hadn't been so late for her tea," retorted Miss Mullen, "Mr. Lambert could have started half an hour before he did."

"Half an hour will be neither here nor there in this game. What Lambert ought to have done was to have started after luncheon, but I think I may remind you, Miss Mullen, that you took him off to the holy well then."

"Well, and if I did, I didn't leave my best pocket handkerchief hanging in rags on the thorn-bush, like some other people I know of!" Miss Mullen felt that she had scored, and looked for sympathy to Pamela, who, having as was usual with her, borne the heat and burden of the day in the matter of packings and washings-up, was now sitting, pale and tired, in the stern, with Dinah solidly implanted in her lap, and Max huddled miserably on the seat beside her. Miss Hope-

Drummond, shrouded in silence and a long plaid
cloak, paid no attention to anyone or anything.
There are few who can drink the dregs of the cup
of pleasuring with any appearance of enjoyment,
and Miss Hope-Drummond was not one of them.
The alteration in the respective crews of the yacht
and the steam-launch had been made by no wish
of hers, and it is probable that but for the unexpected support that Cursiter had received from
Miss Mullen, his schemes for Mr. Hawkins' welfare
would not have prospered.   The idea had indeed
occurred to Miss Hope-Drummond that the pro-
prietor of the launch had perhaps a personal
motive in suggesting the exchange, but when she
found that Captain Cursiter was going to stand
with his back to her, and steer, she wished that
she had not yielded her place in the *Daphne* to a
young person whom she already thought of as
" *that* Miss Fitzpatrick," applying in its full force
the demonstrative pronoun that denotes feminine
animosity more subtly and expressively than is in
the power of any adjective.   Hawkins she felt was
out of her jurisdiction and unworthy of attention,

and she politely ignored Pamela's attempts to in-
volve her in conversation with him. Her neat
brown fringe was out of curl; long strands of hair
blew unbecomingly over her ears; her feet were
very cold, and she finally buried herself to the
nose in a fur boa that gave her the effect of a
moustached and bearded Russian noble, and began,
as was her custom during sermons and other periods
of tedium, to elaborate the construction of a new
tea-gown.

To do Mr. Hawkins justice, he, though equally
ill-treated by fate, rose superior to his disappointment. After his encounter with Miss Mullen he
settled confidentially down in the corner beside
Pamela, and amused himself by pulling Dinah's
short, fat tail, and puffing cigarette smoke in her
face, while he regaled her mistress with an assort-
ment of the innermost gossip of Lismoyle.

On board the *Daphne*, the aspect of things was
less comfortable. Although the wind was too much
in her teeth for her to make much advance for home,
there was enough to drive her through the water at a
pace that made the long tacks from side to side of the

lake seem as nothing, and to give Francie as much as she could do to keep her big hat on her head. She was sitting up on the weather side with Lambert, who was steering ; and Christopher, in the bows, was working the head sails, and acting as movable ballast when they went about. At first, while they were beating out of the narrow channel of Ochery, Francie had found it advisable to lie in a heap beneath a tarpaulin, to avoid the onslaught of the boom at each frequent tack, but now that they were out on the open lake, with the top-sail hoisted, she had risen to her present position, and, in spite of her screams as the sharp squalls came down from the mountains and lifted her hat till it stood on end like a rearing horse, was enjoying herself amazingly. Unlike Miss Hope-Drummond, she was pre-eminently one of those who come home unflagging from the most prolonged outing, and to-day's entertainment, so far from being exhausting, had verified to the utmost her belief in the charms of the British officer, as well as Miss Fanny Hemphill's prophecies of her success in such quarters. Nevertheless she was quite content

to return in the yacht; it was salutary for Mr.
Hawkins to see that she could do without him
very well, it took her from Charlotte's dangerous
proximity, and it also gave her an opportunity
of appeasing Mr. Lambert, who, as she was quite
aware, was not in the best of tempers. So far
her nimble tongue had of necessity been idle.
Christopher's position in the bows isolated him
from all conversation of the ordinary pitch, and
Lambert had been at first too much occupied with
the affairs of his boat to speak to her, but now,
as a sharper gust nearly snatched her hat from
her restraining hand, he turned to her.

"If it wasn't that you seem to enjoy having that
hat blown inside out every second minute," he said
chillingly, "I'd offer to lend you a cap."

"What sort is it?" demanded Francie. "If it's
anything like that old deerstalker thing you have
on your head now, I wouldn't touch it with the
tongs!"

Lambert's only reply was to grope under the
seat with one hand, and to bring out a red knitted
cap of the conventional sailoring type, which he

handed to Francie without so much as looking at her. Miss Fitzpatrick recognised its merits with half a glance, and, promptly putting it on her head, stuffed the *chef d'œuvre* of the night before under the seat among the deck-swabs and ends of rope that lurked there. Christopher, looking aft at the moment, saw the change of head-gear, and it was, perhaps, characteristic of him that even while he acknowledged the appropriateness of the red cap of liberty to the impertinence of the brilliant face beneath it, he found himself reminded of the extra supplement, in colours, of any Christmas number—indubitably pretty but a trifle vulgar.

In the meantime the object of this patronising criticism, feeling herself now able to give her undivided attention to conversation, regarded Mr. Lambert's sulky face with open amusement, and said :

"Well, now, tell me what made you so cross all day. Was it because Mrs. Lambert wasn't out?"

Lambert looked at her for an instant without speaking. "Ready about," he called out. "Mind your head! Lee helm!"

The little yacht hung and staggered for a moment, and then, with a diving plunge, started forward, with every sail full and straining. Francie scrambled with some difficulty to the other side of the tiny cockpit, and climbed up on to the seat by Mr. Lambert, just in time to see a very fair imitation of a wave break on the weather bow and splash a sparkling shower into Christopher's face.

"Oh, Mr. Dysart! are you drowned?" she screamed ecstatically.

"Not quite," he called back, his hair hanging in dripping points on his forehead as he took off his cap and shook the water out of it. "I say, Lambert, it's beginning to blow pretty stiff; I'd take that top-sail off her, if I were you."

"She's often carried it in worse weather than this," returned Lambert; "a drop of water will do no one any harm."

Mr. Lambert in private, and as much as possible in public, affected to treat his employer's son as a milksop, and few things annoyed him more than the accepted opinion on the lake that there was no better man in a boat than Christopher Dysart. His secret fear that it was true made it now all the more intolerable that Christopher should lay down the law to him on a point of seamanship, especially with Francie by, ready in that exasperating way of hers to laugh at him on the smallest provocation.

"It'll do him no harm if he does get a drop of water over him," he said to her in a low voice, forgetting for the moment his attitude of disapproval. "Take some of the starch out of him for once!" He took a pull on the main sheet, and, with a satisfied upward look at the top-sail in question, applied himself to conversation. The episode had done him good, and it was with almost fatherly seriousness that he began :

"Now, Francie, you were telling me a while ago that I was cross all day. I'm a very old friend of yours, and I don't mind saying that I was greatly put out by the way"—he lowered his voice—"by the way you were going on with that fellow Hawkins."

"I don't know what you mean by 'going on,'"

interrupted Francie, with a slight blush. " What's the harm in talking to him if he likes to talk to me ? "

" Plenty of harm," returned Lambert quickly, "when he makes a fool of you the way he did to-day. If you don't care that Miss Dysart and the rest of them think you know no better than to behave like that, *I* do ! "

" Behave like what ? "

" Well, for one thing, to let him and Garry Dysart go sticking grass in your stockings that way after luncheon ; and for another to keep Miss Dysart waiting tea for you for half an hour, and your only excuse to be to tell her that he was 'teaching you to make ducks and drakes' the other side of the island." The fatherly quality had died out of his voice, and the knuckles of the hand that held the tiller grew white from a harder grip.

Francie instinctively tucked away her feet under her petticoats. She was conscious that the green pattern still adorned her insteps, and that tell-tale spikes of grass still projected on either side of her shoes.

"How could I help it? It was just a silly game that he and Garry Dysart made up between them; and as for Miss Dysart being angry with me, she never said a word to me; she was awfully good; and she and her brother had kept the teapot hot for me, and everything." She looked furtively at Christopher, who was looking out at the launch, now crossing their path some distance ahead. It was more than *you'd* have done for me!"

"Yes, very likely it was; but I wouldn't have been laughing at you in my sleeve all the time as they were, or at least as he was, anyhow!"

"I believe that's a great lie," said Francie unhesitatingly; "and I don't care a jack-rat what he thought, or what you think either. Mr. Hawkins is a very nice young man, and I'll talk to him just as much as I like! And he's coming to tea at Tally Ho to-morrow; and what's more, I asked him! So now!"

"Oh, all right!" said Lambert, in such a constrained voice of anger, that even Francie felt a little afraid of him. "Have him to tea by all means; and if I were you I should send down to Limerick and have Miss M'Carthy up to meet him !"

" What are you saying ? Who's Miss M'Carthy ?" asked Francie, with a disappointing sparkle of enjoyment in her eyes.

" She's the daughter of a George's Street tobacconist that your friend Mr. Hawkins was so sweet about a couple of months ago that they packed him off here to be out of harm's way. Look out, Dysart, I'm going about now," he continued without giving Francie time to reply. " Leehelm !"

" Oh, I'm sick of you and your old 'leehelm'!" cried Francie, as she grovelled again in the cockpit to avoid the swing of the boom. " Why can't you go straight like Captain Cursiter's steamer, instead of bothering backwards and forwards, side-ways, like this? And you always do it just when I want to ask you something."

This complaint, which was mainly addressed to Mr. Lambert's canvas yachting shoes, received no attention. When Francie came to the surface she found that the yacht was at a more uncomfortable angle than ever, and with some difficulty she established herself on the narrow strip of deck, outside the coaming, with her feet hanging into the cockpit.

"Now, Mr. Lambert," she began at once, "you'd better tell me Miss M'Carthy's address, and all about her, and perhaps if you're good I'll ask you to meet her too."

As she spoke, a smart squall struck the yacht, and Lambert luffed her hard up to meet it. A wave with a ragged white edge flopped over her bows, wetting Christopher again, and came washing aft along the deck behind the coaming.

"Look out aft there!" he shouted. "She's putting her nose into it! I tell you that top-sail's burying her, Lambert."

Lambert made no answer to either Francie or Christopher. He had as much as he could do to hold the yacht, which was snatching at the tiller like a horse at its bit, and ripping her way deep through the waves in a manner too vigorous to be pleasant. It was about seven o'clock, and though the sun was still some height above the dark jagged wall of the mountains, the clouds had risen in a tawny fleece across his path, and it was evident that he would be seen no more that day. The lake had turned to indigo. The beds of reeds near the shore were pallid by contrast as they stooped under the wind ; the waves that raced towards the yacht had each an angry foam-crest, having, after the manner of lake waves, lashed themselves into a high state of indignation on very short notice, and hissed and effervesced like soda-water all along the lee gunwale of the flying yacht. A few seagulls that were trying to fight their way back down to the sea, looked like fluttering scraps of torn white paper against the angry bronze of the clouds, and the pine trees on the point, under the lee of which they were scudding, were tossing like the black plumes of a hearse.

Lambert put the yacht about, and headed back across the lake.

"We did pretty well on that tack, Dysart," he shouted. "We ought to get outside Screeb Point with the next one, and then we'll get the wind a point fairer, and make better weather of it the rest of the way home."

He could see the launch, half a mile or so beyond the point, ploughing steadily along on her way to Lismoyle, and in his heart he wished that Francie was on board of her. He also wished that Christopher had held his confounded tongue about the top-sail. If he hadn't shoved in his oar where he wasn't wanted, he'd have had that top-sail off her twenty minutes ago; but he wasn't going to stand another man ordering him about in his own boat.

"Look here, Francie," he said, "you must look out for yourself when I'm going about next time. It's always a bit squally round this point, so you'd better keep down in the cockpit till we're well on the next tack."

"But I'll get all wet down there," objected Francie, "and I'd much rather stay up here and see the fun."

"You talk as if it was the top of a tram in Sackville Street," said Lambert, snatching a glance of provoked amusement at her unconcerned face. "I can tell you it will take a good deal more holding on to than that does. Promise me now, like a good child," he went on, with a sudden thrill of anxiety at her helplessness and ignorance, "that you'll do as I tell you. You *used* to mind what I said to you."

He leaned towards her as he spoke, and Francie raised her eyes to his with a laugh in them that made him for the moment forgetful of everything else. They were in the open water in the centre of the lake by this time, and in that second a squall came roaring down upon them.

"Luff!" shouted Christopher, letting go the head sheets. "Luff, or we're over!"

Lambert let go the main sheet and put the tiller hard down with all the strength he was master of, but he was just too late. In that moment, when he had allowed his thoughts to leave his steering, the yacht had dragged herself a thought beyond his control. The rough hand of the wind struck her, and, as she quivered and reeled under the blow, another and fiercer gust caught hold of her, and flung her flat on her side on the water.

Before Christopher had well realised what had happened, he had gone deep under water, come to the surface again, and was swimming, with a

vision before him of a white figure with a red cap
falling headlong from its perch. He raised himself
and shook the water out of his eyes, and swimming a stroke or two to get clear of the mast,
with its sails heaving prone on the water like the
pinions of a great wounded bird, he saw over the
shoulders of the hurrying waves the red cap and
the white dress drifting away to leeward. Through
the noise of the water in his ears, and the confusion of his startled brain, he heard Lambert's
voice shouting frantically he did not know what;
the whole force of his nature was set and centred
on overtaking the red cap to which each stroke
was bringing him nearer and nearer as it appeared
and reappeared ahead of him between the steely
backs of the waves. She lay horribly still, with
the water washing over her face; and as Christopher caught her dress, and turned, breathless, to
try to fight his way back with her to the
wrecked yacht, he seemed to hear a hundred
voices ringing in his ears and telling him that she
was dead. He was a good and practised swimmer,
but not a powerful one. His clothes hung heavily

about him, and with one arm necessarily given to his burden, and the waves and wind beating him back, he began to think that his task was more than he would be able to accomplish. He had up to this, in the intensity of the shock and struggle, forgotten Lambert's existence, but now the agonised shouts that he had heard came back to him, and he raised himself high in the water and stared about with a new anxiety. To his intense relief he saw that the yacht was still afloat, was, in fact, drifting slowly down towards him, and in the water not ten yards from him was her owner, labouring towards him with quick splashing strokes, and evidently in a very exhausted state. His face was purple-red, his eyes half starting out of his head, and Christopher could hear his hard breathing as he slowly bore down upon him.

"She's all right, Lambert!" Christopher cried out, though his heart belied the words. "I've got her! Hold hard; the yacht will be down on us in a minute."

Whether Lambert heard the words or no was not apparent. He came struggling on, and as soon as he got within reach, made a snatch at Francie's dress. Christopher had contrived to get his left arm round her waist, and to prop her chin on his shoulder, so that her face should be above the water, and, as Lambert's weight swung on him, it was all he could do to keep her in this position.

"You'll drown us all if you don't let go!" Uttermost exertion and want of breath made Christopher's voice wild and spasmodic. "Can't you tread water till the boat gets to us?"

Lambert still speechlessly and convulsively dragged at her, his breath breaking from him in loud gasps, and his face working.

"Good God, he's gone mad!" thought Christopher; "we're all done for if he won't let go." In desperation he clenched his fist, with the intention of hitting Lambert on the head, but just as he gathered his forces for this extreme measure something struck him softly in the back. Lambert's weight had twisted him round so that he was no longer facing the yacht, and he did not know how near help was. It was the boom of the *Daphne* that had touched him like a friendly hand, and he turned and caught at it with a feeling of more intense thankfulness than he had known in all his life.

The yacht was lying over on her side, half full of water, but kept afloat by the air-tight compartments that Mrs. Lambert's terrors had insisted on, and that her money had paid for, when her husband had first taken to sailing on the lake. Christopher was able with a desperate effort to get one knee on to the submerged coaming of the cockpit, and catching at its upper side with his right hand, he recovered himself and prepared to draw Francie up after him.

"Come, Lambert, let go!" he said threateningly, "and help me to get her out of the water. You need not be afraid, you can hold on to the boat."

Lambert had not hitherto tried to speak, but now with the support that the yacht gave him, his breath came back to him a little.

"Damn you!" he spluttered, the loud sobbing breaths almost choking him, "I'm not afraid! Let her go! Take your arm from round her, I can hold her better than you can. Ah!" he shrieked, suddenly seeing Francie's face, as Christopher, without regarding what he said, drew her steadily up from his exhausted grasp, "she's dead! you've let her drown!" His head fell forward, and Christopher thought with the calm of despair, " He's going under, and I can't help him if he does. Here Lambert! man alive, don't let go! There! do you hear the launch whistling? They're coming to us!"

Lambert's hand, with its shining gold signet-ring, was gripping the coaming under water with a grasp that was already mechanical. It seemed to Christopher that it had a yellow, drowned look about it. He put out his foot, and, getting it under Lambert's chin, lifted his mouth out of the water. The steam-launch was whistling incessantly, in long notes, in short ones, in jerks, and he lifted up his voice against the forces of the wind and the hissing and dashing of the water to answer her. Perhaps it was the dull weight on his arm and the stricken stillness of the face that lay in utter unconsciousness on his shoulder, but he scarcely recognised his own voice, it was broken with such a tone of stress and horror. He had never before heard such music as Hawkins' shout hailing him in answer, nor seen a sight so heavenly fair as the bow of the *Serpolette* cutting its way through the thronging waves to their rescue. White faces staring over her gunwale broke into a loud cry when they saw him hanging, half-spent, against the tilted deck of the *Daphne.* It was well, he thought, that they had not waited any longer. The only question was whether they were not even now too late. His head swam from excitement and fatigue, his arms and knees trembled, and when at last Francie, Lambert, and finally he himself, were lifted on board the launch, it seemed the culminating point of a long and awful nightmare that Charlotte Mullen should fling herself on her knees beside the bodies of her cousin and her friend, and utter yell after yell of hysterical lamentation.

CHAPTER XV.

"Sausages and bacon, Lady Dysart! Yes, indeed, that was his breakfast, and that for a man who—if you'll excuse the expression, Lady Dysart, but, indeed, I know you're such a good doctor that I'd like you to tell me if it was quite safe—who was vomiting lake water for half an hour after he was brought into the house the night before."

"Do you really mean that he came down to breakfast?" asked Lady Dysart, with the flattering sincerity of interest that she bestowed on all topics of conversation, but specially on those that related to the art and practice of medicine. "He ought to have stayed in bed all day to let the system recover from the shock."|

"Those were the very words I used to him, Lady Dysart," returned Mrs. Lambert dismally; "but indeed all the answer he made was, 'Fiddledc-dee!' He wouldn't have so much as a cup of tea in his bed, and you may think what I suffered, Lady Dysart, when I was down in the parlour making the breakfast and getting his tray ready, when I heard him in his bath overhead— just as if he hadn't been half-drowned the night before. I didn't tell you that, Mrs. Gascogne," she went on, turning her watery gaze upon the thin refined face of her spiritual directress. " Now if it was me such a thing happened to, I'd have that nervous dread of water that I· couldn't look at it for a week."

"No, I am sure you would not," answered Mrs. Gascogne with the over-earnestness which so often shipwrecks the absent-minded; " of course you couldn't expect him to take it if it wasn't made with really boiling water."

Mrs. Lambert stared in stupefaction, and Lady Dysart, far from trying to cloak her cousin's confusion, burst into a delighted laugh.

"Kate! I don't believe you heard a single word that Mrs. Lambert said! You were calculating how many gallons of tea will be wanted for your school feast."

" Nonsense, Isabel ! " said Mrs. Gascogne hotly, with an indignant and repressive glance at Lady Dysart, "and how was it—" turning to Mrs. Lambert, " that he—a—swallowed so much lake water ? "

" He was cot under the sail, Mrs. Gascogne. He made a sort of a dash at Miss Fitzpatrick to save her when she was falling, and he slipped someway, and got in under the sail and he was half-choked before he could get out ! " A tear of sensibility trickled down the good turkey hen's red beak, " Indeed, I don't know when I've been so upset, Lady Dysart," she quavered.

" Upset ! " echoed Lady Dysart, raising her large eyes dramatically to the cut glass chandelier, " I can well believe it ! When it came to ten o'clock and there was no sign of them, I was simply *raging* up and down between the house and the pier like a mad bull robbed of its whelps ! " She turned to Mrs. Gascogne, feeling that there was a biblical ring in the peroration that demanded a higher appreciation than Mrs. Lambert could give, and was much chagrined to see that lady concealing her laughter behind a handkerchief.

Mrs. Lambert looked bewilderedly from one to the other, and, feeling that the ways of the aristocracy were beyond her comprehension, went on with the recital of her own woes.

"He actually went down to Limerick by train in the afternoon—he that was half-drowned the day before, and a paragraph in the paper about his narrow escape. I haven't had a wink of sleep those two nights, what with palpitations and bad dreams. I don't believe, Lady Dysart, I'll ever be the better of it."

"Oh, you'll get over it soon, Mrs. Lambert," said Lady Dysart cheerfully; "why, I had no less than three children—"

"Calves," murmured Mrs. Gascogne, with still streaming eyes.

"Children," repeated Lady Dysart emphatically, "and I thought they were every one of them drowned!"

"Oh, but a *husband*, Lady Dysart," cried Mrs. Lambert with orthodox unction, "what are children compared to the husband?"

"Oh—er—of course not," said Lady Dysart,

with something less than her usual conviction of utterance, her thoughts flying to Sir Benjamin and his bath chair.

"By the way," struck in Mrs. Gascogne, "my husband desired me to say that he hopes to come over to-morrow afternoon to see Mr. Lambert, and to hear all about the accident."

Mrs. Lambert looked more perturbed than gratified. "It's very kind of the Archdeacon I'm sure," she said nervously; "but Mr. Lambert—" (Mrs. Lambert belonged to the large class of women who are always particular to speak of their husbands by their full style and title) "Mr. Lambert is most averse to talking about it, and perhaps—if the Archdeacon didn't mind—"

"That's just what I complain of in Christopher," exclaimed Lady Dysart, breaking with renewed vigour into the conversation. "He was *most* unsatisfactory about it all. Of course, when he came home that night, he was so exhausted that I spared him. I said, 'Not one word will I allow you to say to night, and I *command* you to stay in bed for breakfast to-morrow morning!' I even went down at one o'clock, and pinned a paper on William's door, so that he shouldn't call him. Well—" Lady Dysart, at this turning-point of her story, found herself betrayed into saying "My dear," but had presence of mind enough to direct the expression at Mrs. Gascogne. "Well, my dear, when I went up in the morning, craving for news, he was most confused and unsatisfactory. He pretended he knew nothing of how it had happened, and that after the upset they all went drifting about in a sort of a knot till the yacht came down on top of them. But, of course, something more must have happened to them than *that!* It really was the greatest pity that Miss Fitzpatrick got stunned by that blow on the head just at the beginning of the whole business. *She* would have told us all about it. But men never can describe anything."

"Oh, well, I assure you, Lady Dysart," piped the turkey hen, "Mr. Lambert described to me all that he possibly could, and he said Mr. Dysart gave every assistance in his power, and was the greatest help to him in supporting that poor girl in the water ; but the townspeople were so very inquisitive, and really annoyed him so much with their questions, that he said to me this morning he hoped he'd hear no more about it, which is why I took the liberty of asking Mrs. Gascogne, that the Archdeacon wouldn't mention it to him."

" Oh, yes, yes," said Mrs. Gascogne very politely, recalling herself with difficulty from the mental excursion on which she had started when Lady Dysart's unrelenting eye had been removed. " I am sure he will—a—be delighted. I think, you know, Isabel, we ought—"

Lady Dysart was on her feet in a moment. " Yes, indeed, we ought ! " she responded briskly. " I have to pick up Pamela. Good-bye, Mrs. Lambert; I hope I shall find you looking better the next time I see you, and remember, if you cannot sleep, that there is no opiate like an open window ! "

Mrs. Lambert's exclamation of horror followed her visitors out of the room. Open windows were regarded by her as a necessary housekeeping evil, akin to twigging carpets and whitewashing the kitchen, something to be got over before anyone came downstairs. Not even her reverence for

Lady Dysart would induce her to tolerate such a thing in any room in which she was, and she returned to her woolwork, well satisfied to let the July sunshine come to her through the well-fitting plate-glass windows of her hideous drawing-room.

" The person I do pity in the whole matter," remarked Lady Dysart, as the landau rolled out of the Rosemount gates and towards Lismoyle, " is Charlotte Mullen. Of course, that poor excellent little Mrs. Lambert got a great shock, but that was nothing compared with seeing the sail go flat down on the water, as the people in the launch did. In the middle of all poor Pamela's own fright, when she was tearing open one of the luncheon baskets to get some whisky out, Charlotte went into raging hysterics, and *roared*, my dear! And then she all but fainted on to the top of Mr. Hawkins. Who would ever have thought of her breaking down in that kind of way ? "

" Faugh ! " said Mrs. Gascogne, " disgusting creature ! "

" Now, Kate, you are always saying censorious things about that poor woman. People can't help showing their feelings sometimes, no matter how ugly they are! All that I can tell you is," said Lady Dysart, warming to fervour as was her wont, "if you had seen her this afternoon as I did, with the tears in her eyes as she described the whole thing to me, and the agonies she was in about that girl, you would have felt sorry for her."

Mrs. Gascogne shot a glance, bright with intelligence and amusement, at her cousin's flushed handsome face, and held her peace. With Mrs. Gascogne, to hold her peace was to glide into the sanctuary of her own thoughts, and remain there oblivious of all besides ; but the retribution that would surely have overtaken her at the next pause in Lady Dysart's harangue was averted by the stopping of the carriage at Miss Mullen's gate.

Francie lay back on her sofa after Pamela Dysart had left her. She saw the landau drive away towards Bruff, with the sun twinkling on the silver of the harness, and thought with an ungrudging envy how awfully nice Miss Dysart was, and how lovely it wou d be to have a carriage like that to drive about in. People in Dublin, who were not half as grand as the Dysarts, would have been a great deal too grand to come and see her up in her room like this, but here everyone was as friendly as they could be, and not a bit stuck-up. It was certainly a good day for her when she came down to Lismoyle, and in spite of all that Uncle Robert had said about old Aunt Mullen's money, and how Charlotte had feathered her own nest, there was no denying that Charlotte was not a bad old thing after all. Her only regret was that she had not seen the dress that Miss Dysart had on this afternoon before she had got herself that horrid ready-made pink thing, and the shirt with the big pink horse-shoes on it. Fanny Hemphill's hitherto unquestioned opinion in the matter of costume suddenly tottered in her estimation, and, with the loosening of that buttress of her former life, all her primitive convictions were shaken.

The latch of the gate clicked again, and she leaned forward to see who was coming. "What nonsense it is keeping me up here this way!" she said to herself; "there's Roddy ambert coming in, and won't he be cross when he finds that there's only Charlotte for him to talk to! I *will* come down to-morrow, no matter what they say, but I suppose it will be ages before the officers call again now." Miss Fitzpatrick became somewhat moody at this reflection, and tried to remember what it was that Mr. Hawkins had said about "taking shooting leave for the 12th;" she wished she hadn't been such a fool as not to ask him what he had meant by the 12th. If it meant the 12th of July, she mightn't see him again till he came back, and goodness knows when that would be. Roddy Lambert was all very well, but what was he but an old married man. "Gracious!" she interrupted herself aloud with a little giggle, "how mad he'd be if he thought I called him that!" and Hawkins was really a very jolly fellow. The hall-door opened again; she heard Charlotte's voice raised in leave-taking, and then Mr. Lambert walked slowly down the drive and the hall-door slammed. "He didn't stay long," thought Francie; "I wonder if he's cross because I wasn't downstairs? He's a very cross man. Oh, look at him kicking Mrs. Bruff into the bushes! It's well for him Charlotte's coming upstairs and can't see him!"

Charlotte was not looking any the worse for what she had gone through on the day of the accident; in fact, as she came into the room, there was an air of youthfulness and good spirits about her that altered her surprisingly, and her manner towards her cousin was geniality itself.

·"Well, me child!" she began, "I hadn't a minute since dinner to come and see you. The doorstep's worn out with the world and his wife coming to ask how you are; and Louisa doesn't know whether she's on her head or her heels with all the clean cups she's had to bring in!"

"Well, I wish to goodness I'd been downstairs to help her," said Francie, whirling her feet off the sofa and sitting upright; "there's nothing ails me to keep me stuck up here."

"Well, you shall come down to-morrow," replied Charlotte soothingly; "I'm going to lunch with the Bakers, so you'll have to come down to do your manners to Christopher Dysart. His mother said he was coming to inquire for you to-morrow. And remember that only for him the pike would be eating you at the bottom of the lake this minute! Mind that! You'll have to thank him for saving your life!"

"Mercy on us," cried Francie; "what on earth will I say to him?"

"Oh, you'll find plenty to say to him! They're as easy as me old shoe, all those Dysarts; I'd pity no one that had one of them to talk to, from the mother down. Did you notice at the picnic how Pamela and her brother took all the trouble on themselves? That's what I call breeding, and not sitting about to be waited on like that great lazy hunks, Miss Hope-Drummond! I declare I loathe the sight of these English fine ladies, and my private belief is that Christopher Dysart thinks the same of her, though he's too well-bred to show it. Yes, my poor Susan," fondling with a large and motherly hand the cat that was sprawling on her shoulder; "he's a real gentleman, like yourself, and not a drop of dirty Saxon blood in him. *He* doesn't bring his great vulgar bull-dog here to worry my poor son—"

"What did Mr. Lambert say, Charlotte?" asked Francie, who began to be a little bored by this

rhapsody. " Was he talking about the accident ? "

" Very little," said Charlotte, with a change of
manner; " he only said that poor Lucy, who wasn't
there at all, was far worse than any of us. As I
told him, you, that we thought was dead, would
be down to-morrow, and not worth asking after.
Indeed we were talking about business most of the
time—" She pressed her face down on the cat's
grey back to hide an irrepressible smile of recollection. " But that's only interesting to the parties
concerned."

END OF VOL. I.

Printed by Cowan & Co., Limited, Perth.

WARD & DOWNEY'S NEW BOOKS.

BY WILLIAM O'CONNOR MORRIS.

MOLTKE : A Biographical and Critical Study. Several Portraits, Maps, and Plans of the Principal Battlefields. By His Honour Judge O'CONNOR MORRIS. £1 1s.

"Is not merely a capital sketch of Moltke's great achievements, but a comprehensive review of the wars in which he took a conspicuous part, and of the forces and field officers arrayed on either side."—*Scotsman*.

THE GHOST WORLD. By T. F. THISELTON DYER, Author of "Church Lore Gleanings." 10s. 6d.

"The literature of what may be called ghost-lore is familiar to him. So far as we know, there is no book in our own or any other language which exactly corresponds with Mr. Dyer's book."—*Notes and Queries*.

SOCIAL STUDIES. By LADY WILDE, Author of "Ancient Legends of Ireland." 6s.
"Lady Wilde's 'Social Studies' is a clever book of essays."—*Saturday Review*.

ENLARGED, REVISED, AND CHEAPER EDITION. Now Ready.

ANGELICA KAUFFMANN : a Biograph. With a List of her Paintings and Drawings, and 2 Portraits. By FRANCIS A. GERARD. 1 vol. 6s.
"It is written with kindliness, knowledge, and good taste, and if it contributes little to our knowledge of Angelica Kauffmann as an artist, it helps us materially to understand her versatile charms as woman."—*Standard*.

OUR VIANDS : Whence they Come and How they are Cooked. By A. W. BUCKLAND, Author of "Anthropological Studies." 6s.
"She has succeeded in giving us a very interesting history of our own ordinary dishes and of the most curious and characteristic dishes of other countries."—*Spectator*.

NEW NOVELS NOW READY.

THE QUARRY FARM. By T. S. FLETCHER, Author of "Mr. Spivey's Clerk," "When Charles the First was King," etc. 1 vol., crown 8vo, 6s.

"The story has a charming rural air, and its characters are natural, as well as simple. A reader who likes country stories ought to read this."—*Scotsman*.
"The simplicity and directness of this story will be a surprise to the reader. . . . the tale is certainly very pretty."—*Liverpool Mercury*.

THE TWILIGHT OF LOVE. Being Four Studies of the Artistic Temperament. By CHARLES H. BROOKFIELD. Price 3s. 6d.

"One is charmed throughout with the profound knowledge of human nature, the keenly humorous, even where scornful, appreciation of character, and the terse, bright style of the author."—*Saturday Review*.

MR. JOCKO. By J. FOGERTY, Author of "Countess Irene," etc. With Illustrations. New Edition. 6s.

"The subordinate characters in this powerful novel are sketched with masterly vigour and picturesqueness. . . . . Tobias Miles and Betsy Clinker are veritable *chefs d'œuvres* of characterisation."—*Daily Telegraph*.

BY A HIMALAYAN LAKE. By "AN IDLE EXILE," Author of "In Tent and Bungalow." 3s. 6d.

"The picture of Anglo-Indian Society, with its lights and shadows, is done with an admirably light and effective touch, and the dialogue is both natural and crisp. Altogether a clever, bright book."—*Pall Mall Gazette*.

CPSIA information can be obtained
at www.ICGtesting.com
Printed in the USA
BVHW040614210620
581953BV00007B/663

9 781314 391510